Marry a Pregnant Virgin

FRANK G. HONEYCUTT

Marry a Pregnant Virgin

*Unusual Bible Stories for New
and Curious Christians*

Augsburg Books

MINNEAPOLIS

Marry a Pregnant Virgin
Unusual Bible Stories for New and Curious Christians

© 2008 Augsburg Books, an imprint of Augsburg Fortress.

Visit www.augsburgfortress.org/copyrights/contact.asp or write to Permissions, Augsburg Fortress, Publishers, Box 1209, Minneapolis, MN 55440-1209.

Scripture quotations are taken from The New Revised Standard Version of the Bible, © 1989, by the Division of Christian Education of the National Council of the Churches of Christ in the United States of America. All rights reserved. Used by permission.

Cover image: Anton Raphael Mengs (1728–1779), *Dream of Saint Joseph*,
ca. 1773–74. Kunsthistorisches Museum, Vienna, Austria.
Photo © Erich Lessing/Art Resource, NY. Used by permission.
Cover design: The Design Works Group, Charles Brock
Interior design: Trio Bookworks, Ann Delgehausen

Library of Congress Cataloging-in-Publication Data
Honeycutt, Frank G., 1957–
Marry a pregnant virgin : unusual Bible stories for new and curious
Christians / Frank G. Honeycutt.
p. cm.
Includes bibliographical references.
ISBN 978-0-8066-8036-1 (alk. paper)
1. Bible stories, English. I. Title.
BS550.3.H66 2008
220.6—dc22
2007036817

The paper used in this publication meets the minimum requirements of American National Standard for Information Sciences—Permanence of Paper for Printed Library Materials, ANSI Z329.48-1984.

Manufactured in the U.S.A.

12   11   10   09   08   1   2   3   4   5   6   7   8   9

For Cindy,

as we celebrate twenty-five years

Contents

EASTER

TIME AFTER PENTECOST

Introduction

"I thought that for me he would surely come out, and stand and
call on the name of the Lord his God, and would wave his hand
over the spot, and cure the leprosy!" (2 Kings 5:11)

ONE OF THE REASONS I LOVE THE BIBLE SO MUCH IS THAT IT'S
just a weird book, absolutely wallowing in ambiguity, paradox, and
double entendre. A person who likes things crystal-clear and tied up
with a neat spiritual bow will soon give up on the Bible, because often
it's about as clear as mud on first reading. Always a shocker for the
biblical novice and the many adult catechumens and church "return-
ees" I've worked with is this daunting realization: faithful interpretation of God's word is more often than not an intentionally befuddling
enterprise. "For the Rabbis and Church Fathers," writes Burton
Visotsky, "reading the Book was an adventure, a journey to a grand
palace with many great and awesome halls, banquet rooms, and
chambers, as well as many passages and locked doors. The adventure
lay in learning the secrets of the palace, unlocking all the doors and
perhaps catching a glimpse of the King in all his splendor."[1]

Early in his career, the prophet Ezekiel heard the divine voice telling him to "Eat this scroll that I give you and fill your stomach with
it" (3:3). In other words, go swallow some scripture for lunch. Such
odd dietary advice surely means that someone presuming to speak
for God must chew on the Bible with measured and slow scriptural
mastication, turning the story over and over, admiring it like a fine
jewel. In this process of turning and examining, the story begins to
gestate and take root in the imagination. But this obviously requires
both time and patience, which is precisely why so many of us modern people, including weekly churchgoers, do not read the Bible with
any regularity. We like our spiritual truths served up quickly with
sitcom clarity. We prefer the condensed version, *God's Little Devotional Bible*, the easy path to insight—a straight, unencumbered

shortcut to divine wisdom. Americans largely choose television over slowly distilled truth.

Jesus' disciples once wondered why he so often taught in parables, stories whose meanings weren't at all obvious on first hearing. He oddly enough confessed to telling parables so that looking, people "may *not* perceive, and listening, they may *not* understand" (Luke 8:10). Now what is that? You'd think the Savior of the world would want instant and obvious clarity, but instead he purposefully constructs his stories to confuse and leave us would-be disciples scratching our heads. Jesus was about the regular business of intentional obfuscation. That, in a word, is weird. And that is one reason I love the Bible so much. It makes me dig. And think. Given perceived time restraints, it's always tempting to rely on a spiritual guru for *ex cathedra* pronouncements instead of doing the hard work of theological reflection for myself. As George Gallup Jr. once noted, "The problem isn't that Americans don't believe in anything; it's that they believe in *everything*."

Please notice—*Jesus would not spell it all out for his followers.* He taught in an elliptical fashion, "to be continued" in the hearts and minds of his listeners, the truth of the story often detonating days later. New Christians may find this strange, but it is also smart. "The Bible may be difficult and confusing," Thomas Merton wrote, "but it is meant to challenge our intelligence, not insult it. It becomes insulting when it is distorted by fanaticism and foolish religiosity."[2] Jesus wisely told theologically dense stories that made people scratch their heads. Where did he learn to teach this way? Precisely from the old stories he was told over and again as a child around home and hearth—stories that began to work on a listener over holy, percolated, and unhurried time. Stories like this one—a classic interpretive knuckleball that floats in various directions simultaneously.

Once upon a time there was a man called Naaman. A great military warrior, he was probably our equivalent of a decorated general—a proud man who was fairly well-off and filled his den with memorabilia from past battles. One rather odd detail from his military résumé is that even though he was a foreigner, an Aramean, a Syrian, Naaman's services were once used by the God of Israel to defeat his own people (2 Kings 5:1). God sometimes got miffed with the chosen ones and used foreign mercenaries to slap the homeboys around a bit. Strange, I'll admit, but there are several instances of this in the Old Testament. God was not above consorting with the enemy to get the attention of his chosen.

Well, General Naaman had a problem. He had leprosy. Was that his main problem? (I'll leave that for you to decide, but be thinking about the question.) Anyway, the leprosy bugged him, tormented the proud man. His wife's maid (an Israelite POW-slave girl) knew of a man called Elisha back home who might be able to help Naaman, so the general packs up an impressive caravan and heads to the Promised Land with a letter of royal recommendation. What did this man of means take with him? Ten talents of silver, six thousand shekels of gold, and ten sets of the finest men's clothing money could buy (5:5). The silver, according to a note in my *Oxford Annotated NRSV*, weighed about 750 pounds and the gold about 150 pounds. That's a lot of glittering loot (and enough threads to keep the people at Land's End hopping for weeks)—all for the prophet Elisha, friend of she-bears (2:24) and retriever of buoyant ax-heads (6:6); the holy man who did not keep a whole lot hanging in his closet. Well before the days of Blue Cross/Blue Shield, Naaman was amply prepared to purchase his health care and also slip the healer a sport coat under the table.

So here's the picture: Naaman finally locates Elisha's house. The chariots, the gold, the silver, the sport coats, and the whole military entourage come rolling to a stop at the prophet's front door. Perhaps there was a trumpet flourish to announce Naaman's arrival—pomp, circumstance, and enough military hoo-ha to make Colin Powell blush. The dust settles and a messenger finally emerges from Elisha's front door. He hands Naaman a note. The handlers of this proud man are puzzled and quiet as the message slowly sinks in.

The leprous general hits the roof. "Go wash seven times in that excuse for a river? I thought that for me, *for me* after all, he would surely come out and wave his hand over the spot and cure the leprosy! *Does he know who I am?* He could at least have said *abracadabra* or something." Naaman is riled, absolutely furious. His whole sense of importance, entitlement, and significance is called into question by this flippant advice to go wash in some second-rate river. Naaman turns, perhaps gives Elisha the equivalent of the "Aramean finger," and storms off. It was like he'd been told to "Go and do seven hand-stands" or "Jump rope for a minute while holding your breath." Elisha didn't even bother to come out and greet the general. He sent a preposterous prescription. No one brushes off this man of means and gets away with it.

But cooler heads prevail in the story. And Generalissimo Naaman is finally healed. Isn't this a rich image of the proud general dipping himself seven times (5:14) in a muddy river? The general is healed of his affliction, yes—that's one level of the story. But is that the real point of this old tale? What really needed healing in Naaman's life? Is this story centrally about leprosy at all? Or is it more about an "inner leprosy" in Naaman—a certain pride and arrogance that is even harder to heal?

Very often the Bible will tell a story that seems to be about one thing when actually it's a curve ball about something else entirely. Very often we expect God to be about one thing (healing the body, for example) but God instead works powerfully in a way other than the expected or requested. Very often we want instant healing of what's skin-deep ("I thought that surely *for me* God would wave his hand!"), but instead God goes much deeper and gets at the inner leprosy that so often afflicts our faith and trust. Very often we expect the dramatic and the obvious and the "golly-gee" from God, while God has bigger (but more subtle) fish to fry in our lives, far below the surface.

C. S. Lewis, in one of his classic tales of Narnia, *The Silver Chair*, leads the reader on a dark, circuitous journey that is largely underground. Aslan appears to Jill Pole, a young girl about to depart for this unknown, subterranean land. Before Jill sets out with her companions, Aslan offers this ominous advice which sounds a bit like the great *shema* (literally "hear" in Hebrew) from Deuteronomy 6:4-9[3]: "Remember, remember, remember the Signs. Say them to yourself when you wake in the morning and when you lie down at night, and when you wake in the middle of the night. And whatever strange things may happen to you, let nothing turn your mind from following the Signs. . . . And the Signs which you have learned here will not look at all as you expect them to look, when you meet them there. That is why it is so important to know them by heart and pay no attention to appearances. Remember the Signs and believe the Signs. Nothing else matters."[4] There are odd, seemingly tangential details in the journey of biblical study that matter mightily—scraps of bread, sips of wine, strange and baffling signs along the way. No shortcuts allowed. "Pay no attention to appearances."

When we read this old story about Naaman and his leprosy *quickly*, it first seems to be about the dramatic healing of somebody in a health fix. And maybe we are left wondering why God does not still act in this headline-grabbing way with us. The interpretive twist here is a subtle parody that serves as a mirror reflecting our own impatience with God, whose "thoughts are not our thoughts" (Isaiah 55:8) and whose ways (and Bible) seem absurd. Any enterprise "able to judge the thoughts and intentions of the heart" (Hebrews 4:12) will require blocks of unhurried and reflective time.

Many years later, centuries later, in his hometown of Nazareth, Jesus preached a sermon (Luke 4:27) based upon this same story from Second Kings. And after they heard it, his irate childhood neighbors ran the preacher out of town. Jesus went in a different direction in his sermon about Naaman that day to illustrate the radical inclusion of the gospel, but such an interpretive turn illustrates my point precisely. These old stories are like fine jewels—our job is to turn them over and over, slowly and with much patience and care, and see where they shine and lead us.

Of course, not every interpretation is equally valid. I remember a line in a Reynolds Price novel where one character offers a remark accusing his friend's father (who is a pastor) of seeing a sermon almost anywhere, even "in a pile of dog do."[5] In Christian community, we are blessed with interpretive limits. But if Martin Luther was right about the "living word," part of the beauty of the Bible for befuddled newcomers to church life is that we are far from exhausting the truth in these old texts even after centuries of reflection. Walter Cronkite's voice in the old television series, "And You Are There," still rings in the ears of a careful interpreter of the Bible.

I offer the essays that follow, arranged around the gift and structure of the church year, with new Christians in mind—particularly those who are learning new skills of interpretation in tackling old and timeless stories of the Bible. Long-time church members sometimes forget how strange and confusing biblical narrative can be for newcomers.[6] Therefore, pastors, faith formation teams, and other curious Christians interested in welcoming new disciples into the life of the congregation will also benefit from these reflections. I have tried to embrace each Bible story from the interpretive perspective of wonder and playful curiosity, keeping clearly in mind those who may be leaving a fairly recent theological stance of agnosticism or even atheism. Since conversion is rarely an "all at once" enterprise, Christian hospitality will always attempt to take seriously the questions that linger long after one first enters the doors of a church building. Authentic evangelism requires loving accompaniment and gospel patience.

"Eat this book," God told Ezekiel long ago.

What a feast. What a menu for a world starved for nourishing stories of deliverance and divine purpose. In an era of much spiritual hand waving, no other diet can touch the Bible for real and lasting healing.

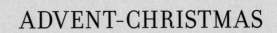

ADVENT-CHRISTMAS

Advent-Christmas

In the fourteenth century the mystic Catherine of Siena wrote a poem in which she describes the Holy Trinity's infatuation with human beings. She refers to the high, eternal God as one absolutely "drunk with love." In Advent, we celebrate the repeated coming of such a God into our past, present, and future—especially realized in the rather intoxicating gift of Jesus, whose incarnation at Christmas was planned from the dawn of time (see Colossians 1:15-20).

My favorite story of this season describes pregnant Mary's journey to see her pregnant relative, Elizabeth, in the hill country. These two women—one young, one old—share conversation, stories, and songs about God around the kitchen table (along with a cup of hot tea, I like to think). Mary stays three solid months for a good long visit (Luke 1:39-56). There is nothing rushed. The conversation is both rich and full. They are completely attentive to one another and the presence of a "drunken" God in their lives who is doing new and marvelous things.

We are in deep need of such unhurried time to celebrate and ponder the advent of God (the word "adventure" is related) in our own lives. How shall we offer our full-bodied attention to God in response to the gift of incarnation? The ancient Advent wreath hearkens from a time when Scandinavian farmers prepared for winter in the year's waning light. They would bring one cartwheel into the house and decorate the wheel with candles and greenery. The message was clear: you can't go anywhere on three wheels. The world was slowing down, a spiritual cue for all God's people. Every Advent, I've been tempted to remove a tire from my trusty Mitsubishi Mirage and adorn the wheel in a similar way. That might finally slow me down a bit.

A slower Advent pace is not easy in a world filled with so many distractions. Spirituality with any depth is frankly a lot of hard work and will require plenty of time, just like any good relationship. In the Advent and Christmas seasons, we celebrate how God has vowed to reach us with a "drunken love." It is only fitting that we also get specific as to how we might regularly reach back.

1

Desert Highway Home

ISAIAH 40:1-11

I remember a very wet day in the fall of 1980. Nearing the town of Kent, Connecticut, on the Appalachian Trail, hiking alone from Maine to Georgia, I walked through sheets of rain, absolutely soaked from head to toe. It was a nice feeling knowing that I would soon be out of the weather in a boarding house in town—doing laundry, taking a shower, maybe eating some pizza.

But somehow on that very wet day I missed a turn in the trail. Coming upon a clearing in the woods at the top of a mountain, there was a rock painted with a short white line. On one side of the line were the capital letters CT—on the other side, the letters NY. In the driving rain and in my eagerness to get dry, I'd crossed into the state of New York without knowing it, several miles out of my way. I was horribly turned around and now faced a much longer and wetter day than first planned. Standing there soaked to the bone, alone on the state line, I offered a loud and echoing expletive that nobody but God heard.

∘ ∘ ∘

Have you ever been lost? Really and truly lost? The Bible speaks of geographical dislocation, but more often than not depicts people who get turned around in a metaphorical sense—people who lose their way in life, people who make mistakes and get off track. Sometimes our decisions and actions have very real consequences that do not allow a quick or clear recovery. I spent a summer as a prison chaplain. In that place was the palpable absence of hope, no way to mend what had been done. Years stretched out ahead in a futureless limbo. It is a lonely, isolating feeling to be that lost.

Maybe not a prisoner in the literal sense, but I suspect you know someone who has lost their way, who has messed up in a fashion that has brought profound consequences. Perhaps you are dealing with something in your own life that is so troubling and upsetting that the road ahead seems utterly blocked and muddied, and you're just unable to move forward. We all get lost in this life, in a wilderness without clear maps; we shout expletives into the darkness that only God can hear.

In the Old Testament, there are two core events that color the whole corpus of books we fondly refer to as the OT. There's more to the Hebrew Bible than these two events, but if you keep these two in mind as you read, you will stay oriented; you'll understand two of the key dynamics of our life with God. The first event is the exodus, which conjures other words like slavery and bondage, liberation and freedom. I refer to the exodus as an "event" and it is that, but it's also a movement—a continuing action in the lives of the people of God. Don't get hung up on the paranormal parting of the Red Sea and how that could have possibly happened. Think instead of how God's divine intent is *always* inclined toward freedom and liberation. The theological stamp of the exodus is all through the Bible and clearly colors the Christian sacraments. In baptism, we pass through the waters and are washed up on dry ground as new people. In Holy

Communion, our sins are "passed over" because the blood of Christ on a cross adorns the lintel of our lives. Watch for exodus themes in your reading: the liberation of enslaved people from situations beyond their control.

There is a second major event in the Old Testament that colors the theological imagination of God's people—the exile into Babylon in 587 BC. Whereas the exodus is about liberation from events beyond our human control, the exile can be directly linked to the rebellion and disobedience of the Israelite people. The prophets warned them; the people ignored the prophets. God gave repeated chances; these chances fell on deaf ears. God's people were carted away to Babylon after the fall of Jerusalem. They had no one to blame but themselves. The years stretched out before them: a futureless limbo with Jerusalem in ruins. This was a time of great hopelessness. Watch for themes of exile in your reading in both testaments: theological consequences coming home to roost in the lives of disobedient people.

Isaiah 40 opens with an announcement that the exile is over. "Comfort, comfort my people." Even though this is a rather famous Bible passage (appearing in Handel's *Messiah*), it's also a rather confusing one due to the difficulty of determining just who is speaking where. Here's a quick key to the biblical score—verses 1–2 are the voice of God announcing the conclusion of the exile. "She has served her term. The penalty is paid, the incarceration over. Comfort these people."

In verses 3 through the first five words of verse 6, "a voice" announces the heavenly construction of a desert highway that will lead the exiles home. Now who is this voice? In the New Testament, John the Baptist is interestingly called "the voice." But here the voice is the heavenly court of God announcing the good news. That mountain looming in an exile's life? The long shadow of disobedience? *Leveled.* The rough places of your past? *Smoothed out.* The main message here can be captured in two words: *Come home.* God is building a highway home for people who have screwed up their lives.

It's not until verse 6 that the prophet actually speaks. And it shouldn't come as a surprise that the prophet, who's experienced the exile, isn't all that sure about these promises. The prophet seems a little jaded, somewhat sassy. "Cry? *What shall I cry?*" Exile was no walk in the park. "You want me to tell these folk they have any hope? Here's what they can hope for: life that fades like a flower. Life that's here and gone like so much dry grass." Verse 8, probably offered by the heavenly court, acknowledges our common mortality but confesses God's timeless promise: "the word of God will stand forever."

A vitally important part of ministry for Christian disciples is to announce God's "welcome home" for those who have gotten lost in this life. And even beyond that, to help build a highway in the desert for people who have been in exile—not just people mired in unfortunate circumstances who arouse our compassion, but also people who are *guilty*, people who have done things, perhaps horrible things, and face the consequences of their actions every day. Advent is about echoing God's gracious announcement to people who don't deserve it: *Come home.*

o   o   o

On a recent December Thursday afternoon, near sunset, I drove down to the Congaree River (which runs through the middle of my city) for a walk. I had a little time before a 5:30 meeting and needed to get out of the church building. We have amazing sunsets in South Carolina. The colors in December on the afternoon horizon are simply spectacular.

I crossed the footbridge below the water plant and turned right. The ruins of the closed penitentiary cast a shadow across the water; the high crow's nest of the prison was now empty. People jogged and walked along the path between canal and river—young couples with children, people getting off work, college students, older folk who wanted to stop and chat. It was a nice view in the light of the setting sun: a long line of people moving along the water, way around a bend as far as I could see.

Shortly into my walk, I noticed something I'd never seen in downtown Columbia—there was a deer, alone, trapped in the narrow area between the iron fence and the canal. Back and forth it ran in terror along the rocks, desperate for an exit, lunging repeatedly and violently through the narrow slats in the fence, head thrust between the bars. Several of us helplessly watched its frantic escape attempts until the animal finally fled upstream, its hooves clattering on the rocks.

o   o   o

Are congregations looking in the right places for lost people who might be welcomed home? Are we waiting to invite only those whose lives are fairly together, who might fit into our church communities?

Maybe it was the light. Maybe it was the long line of people who walked together along the water in the shadow of an old prison. Maybe it was a terrified and trapped animal searching for a way out. But for just a moment, a fleeting moment amid this desperation, I seemed to hear a voice rise in a clarity that must have been meant for me, for us: Comfort, O comfort my people, says your God. Speak tenderly to Jerusalem, and cry to her that she has served her term, that her penalty is paid.

For Reflection and Discussion

- *Describe the main differences between "exodus" and "exile." Begin to think of people (possibly yourself) who may fit into one biblical reality or another.*

- *What would need to happen for a congregation to become a place where all people are welcomed, regardless of background or past?*

- *In what specific (perhaps neglected) places might congregations look for "lost" people searching for a new highway home?*

Becoming

LUKE 1:57-80

NOT LONG AGO I WAS prowling around in some old files and ran across a remarkable newspaper clipping from *The Washington Post* that gave an account of Nelson Mandela's release from a South African prison in 1990 after more than twenty-five years as a political prisoner in his own country. The article describes Mandela in the last lingering moments before prison guards brought news of his long-awaited freedom.

A reporter describes Mandela's reaction after finally receiving the word. "[Officials reminded him] that it was past time to leave. . . . At one point, he went into a back room, the room where he had slept, to see if he had left anything. For some reason he just sat down on the bed. Winnie Mandela, his wife, came in to see what he was doing. He got up. They embraced. And tears came rolling down his face. 'Even leaving jail can be difficult,' he says. He held her close and she cried too. . . . Then they slowly walked back out and drank more tea before Mandela said good-bye to his jailers and got into a silver Toyota for the ride to the prison gate."[7]

There is a certain safety in routine, an abiding comfort in order, something altogether calming about our habits. Even in the midst of chaos, I am able to jot down a long list of things to do and I immediately feel better. Making lists gives me a semblance of control over a world gone haywire. My mother tells me that as a child I used to take all of my Christmas presents and stack them neatly under my bed. I would unwrap and place them in line under the lower bunk, never waiting for the wrapping paper to collect and sit around all morning. I was five. That is sick.

Because routine provides us with a certain sense of control and comfort, it is often hard to break out of the habits that have worked for us for years. Those habits make it difficult to be spontaneous and sense something new afoot in our lives, difficult to leave the safety of prescribed order. Even Nelson Mandela felt something of this as he sat on a prison bunk, waiting to be released. There is a great and powerful tug in our lives to simply continue on, year after year, with what has worked. And maybe the routine really isn't working so well, come to think of it, but it just seems so much easier to stay the course and not rock the boat or ruffle feathers or have loved ones worry that you're going off the deep end. So months or even years pass and we're feeling this gnawing sense to change something, but it's just easier— so much easier, we think—to stay the course and live with the inertia that will indeed carry us along if we don't think about it too much. Just go with the flow, go with what has worked in the past.

C. S. Lewis once wrote that all human beings have a deep, unquenchable yearning. No one is exempt. Lewis used the German term *Sehnsucht* to describe "this pressing, restless longing for fulfillment that nothing can satisfy more than temporarily."[8]

Lewis suggests that humans tend to handle this deep yearning, this restless hunger, in three different ways. The first person, lovingly called a "fool" by Lewis, believes the yearning can be satisfied through the attainment of a particular goal. But upon reaching the goal, one discovers that it doesn't satisfy for very long. Lewis suggests that many people are caught in an endless cycle of striving for inappropriate goals that never satisfy, "jumping from one inadequate goal to another." Lewis calls this person a "fool" because the whole of life is dedicated to achieving goals that are ultimately empty and meaningless. (Unfortunately, it is very easy to detect this in others but much harder to see in ourselves.)

In contrast, the "sensible" person, according to Lewis, feels this deep yearning and is quite aware of its tug on his or her life, but spends all of life trying to push it under, hoping it will go away. It never does go away, of course, but we become experts at avoiding the yearning or pretending it isn't really there. We try to suppress this gnawing tug but it keeps surfacing, trying to get our attention.

Lewis goes on to describe a third way. He says that if we simply cannot satisfy this insatiable yearning through goals or bouncing from one unhealthy itch to the next, and if we cannot ultimately succeed in suppressing the longing by pushing it under, then something else must be true. "We must realize," he concludes, "that we are made for another world."

He doesn't mean that we should try to escape this world and instantly hope for heaven. He means that this yearning that we all feel (but seem unable to follow) doesn't have its origins in the world as we know it. The yearning is essentially for a world quite different from this one where all are fed, welcomed, housed, loved, and honored. We are not made for *this* world. We are made for *that* world. Thus our deep yearning that won't go away. Lewis says that until we recognize this and open our lives fully to God who seeks to bring that world into this one, we will bounce endlessly and unhealthily between urges that never satisfy (I'm sure you can name a few) or we will forever suppress the built-in longing in the name of fear or security or plain old routine.

Now that is a rather long introduction to an Advent story describing the birth of John the Baptist. I spend some time leading up to the story because there are quite a few forces at work in this old tale that are the very same forces, the same old inertia, that invite us to feed the deep yearning unhealthily, or simply suppress and ignore it in the name of routine. Let me name a few.

First, this couple is old. Zechariah and Elizabeth are no spring chickens. Zechariah has no doubt been looking at his pension income for retired priests and thinking more and more about that little condo on the coast where he can indeed "coast" until God calls him home. They are perhaps on cruise-control, this couple. But God interrupts these plans with news that Zechariah's octogenarian wife is pregnant. Something new is happening. God, apparently, does not care for cruise-control at any age.

So this story asks an unsettling question: *Are we sliding through life striving for as little inconvenience as possible or are we open to God's upside-down wackiness at any age?* We are made for another world. And if that is true, what does age have to do with our hesitations and plans in this world?

Second, there is certain inertia built in to this particular faith community that this story unmasks. John is born to an old woman and a mute priest. Eight days later it's time to name the boy, and the neighborhood arrives with their knives sharpened for the circumcision. Do you see the safety net of routine at work here? "None of your relatives has this name," they object. It's always been done this way, not that way. Zechariah has to grab a writing tablet to convince these pushy people that God is doing a new thing. HIS NAME IS JOHN. And so the story asks another unsettling question: *What forces of cultural routine seek to derail and manage God in our lives?* We are made for another world. And if that is true, whose voice really captivates our attention? Finally, the neighbors get the idea that these two old parents are listening to a voice they've never heard. Fear comes over them. They sense the disruption of the normal. And so the community asks what I think is the most poignant question in the entire book of Luke: *What then will this child become?*

And I'm sure Luke was thinking about baby John and even baby Jesus six months later. But Luke was also thinking of you and me. "What then will this child become?"

So what do you think? What's in store up ahead? There are many forces that stand in the way of our "becoming." Many forces in the neighborhood of our lives that seek to help us satisfy the yearning for God inappropriately, or suppress the yearning for God unsuccessfully. "Even leaving jail can be difficult," said Nelson Mandela.

What then will this child become?

For Reflection and Discussion

- *Try to describe a time (like Nelson Mandela) when you knew it was time to leave a certain place in your life, but the lure of routine delayed or shaped the change.*

- *Summarize and comment upon the three types of people described by C. S. Lewis. Do these descriptions seem complete to you?*

- *Ponder the question posed in the essay: "What forces of cultural routine seek to derail and manage God in our lives?"*

Wilderness Bypass

LUKE 3:1-7

LOOK CLOSELY IN THE early pages of his gospel and you'll notice that Luke takes special pains to mention seven powerful men— Tiberius, Pilate, Herod, Philip, Lysanias, Annas, and Caiaphas. Luke essentially begins with the film credits. Why does he do this? These names don't mean much to us now, but twenty centuries ago these were the people who made all the headlines. These were the guys on CNN and "Larry King Live" and even "Late Night with David Letterman." They controlled all aspects of politics and religion.

Tiberius, the first one mentioned in the long list, was emperor of the Roman Empire. In AD 29 he controlled well over one million square miles of territory. If you imagine his royal bedroom as the center of this vast empire, Tiberius could have walked a thousand miles out his back door in any direction and still call it his backyard.

Tiberius inherited all this land from his stepfather, the great Caesar Augustus. Tiberius was like a god. No, he *was* "God." People were expected to worship, literally, the very ground he walked on.

The next four guys were his head underlings; they had power, but over less acreage. And the last two, Annas and Caiaphas, oversaw the intricate religious structure in Jerusalem, a structure that had largely lost its way—corrupt but still powerful and wielding a good bit of control over your life if you were a practicing Jew. We don't hear from these seven that much in the Bible. (Pilate and Caiaphas, of course, will resurface when Jesus stands trial.) But all seven were household names in the first century. Luke is throwing around names that had at least as much recognition and power as George Bush, Condoleezza Rice, Donald Rumsfeld, and Billy Graham have today. The seven men listed here were the power elite of Luke's day— lots of money, lots of influence, lots of perks.

But notice: Luke is crystal-clear. The word of God bypasses these seven. They were in charge and Luke knew that. Everybody knew that. But the word of God doesn't come to these seven famous, powerful guys. Instead, God's word rests upon John the Baptist, a "nobody" out in the middle of nowhere whose mother and father (Elizabeth and Zechariah—see previous essay) were so old when John was born that they had to use walking canes to stroll the baby around the block. Without saying so overtly, Luke is making a rather loud theological statement in these first two verses of chapter 3.

God's word bypasses the powerful and rests upon a nobody. I'm not saying that all powerful people are bad people. I am saying that too much power and influence can lead a person, then or now, to conclude that he or she doesn't really need God. Or maybe needs God just as a "divine mascot" to bless occasional situations. But here's a little secret. *God cannot be born where there is no room.* That was true of Bethlehem, true of Tiberius, and it's true of our own lives. God cannot be born where there is no room.

One of the things that John the Baptist says in this old Advent story is, "Prepare the way." God needs room to work, a "way" in your life and mine, space to get at us. Lacking a vacancy, God's word bypasses people no matter their credentials or name recognition or number of years as a church member. There's just no room. Fill your days with noise and appointments and God can *break* your window tapping with the word, but to no avail. God's word bypassed the most powerful people in the world—not because God didn't love them but because their attention was held completely by other callers. So where does God's word finally find a home? With John, yes, but where is he? John is in the wilderness. The Bible is full of stories of people in the wilderness. There is something highly suggestive and theological about such a place. Theology and geography are often close cousins in the Bible.

If you've ever visited a wilderness area, you know that there are no directional or mileage signs, minimal trail maintenance, and no human structures of any kind. And best of all no noise, except the wind and snapping twigs as one walks. Some wilderness areas have even protected the air space surrounding the acreage from airline flight patterns. The Bible's use of this word with John the Baptist suggests that such a place is where God's word will also find us.

I think we can create "wilderness" spaces in our own homes where we can encounter God's word without interruption, without distraction, in solitude. We don't have to answer every ringing telephone. The television or radio doesn't always have to be on as background noise. God needs room, space in our lives. Lacking such, God's word may bypass the busy and distracted.

At any baptism parents and sponsors make specific promises on behalf of a child. They will promise, among other things, to bring this child to worship, teach her the traditions of the church, convey to him the great stories of the Bible. Why do we bother with these promises anyway? Why not just pour the water and say the words? Because God needs room to work in a new disciple's life and in all of our lives. God cannot wiggle a divine nose and say, "Poof, you're a mature Christian." God needs room, space, to be born in our lives.

This is undeniably one of the great challenges facing the church in a new century. We often lack the consistent spiritual discipline allowing God to get at us. Every Sunday in my own denomination, for example, *two-thirds* of our five million members are absent from worship. What kind of message are we sending God with these figures?

In my files I've saved a wonderful article (written by Barbara Brown Taylor) about the loss of languages in our world. She reports that of the six thousand languages in the world today, about half will probably die out in this new century. There are a variety of reasons for the loss of these languages including modern communications, human migration, and population growth. Children are less interested in learning the ways and tongues of their forebears.

Taylor connects this reality to our own Christian faith, her own Christian language. "Many of our grandchildren," she says, "have no interest in learning what sounds to them like primitive speech. . . . It is not impossible to imagine the day when some ancestor [*sic*] of mine will read an obituary that announces, 'Alma Johnson, 76, Dies, and Christian Tongue with her.'" Taylor concludes with an ominous observation: "If we want [our language] to live, then we must somehow convince our children to speak it—either by requiring them to learn it the same way we require them to learn English or Spanish, or by introducing them to realities so holy that they beg to know what such things are called."[9]

Seven VIPs—the most powerful people in the world. The word of God bypassed them all. Not because God wouldn't speak it but because they couldn't hear it—too many distractions, not enough room.

One person. Out in the wilderness. Speaking a language of redemption and hope that would change the world.

It's a pretty clear choice we have.

For Reflection and Discussion

- *What is revealed about a God who "cannot be born where there is no room"?*

- *Reflect upon your own typical day or week. How could you create your own "wilderness area" in the regular rhythms of your life?*

- *If you are new at learning the "language" of the Christian faith, what could you tell church leaders that might assist them in helping you learn the language?*

4

Surrogate Messiahs

John 1:19-28

THE religious leaders who wander out into the wilderness to check on John must be getting a little frustrated. The ecclesiastical vanguard from the big city has commissioned a fact-finding team to interview this man who wears little more than a camel's hair windbreaker and dines on honey and bugs. Mystics and eccentrics have always made mainline religious leaders rather nervous. The fact finders stand there on the banks of the Jordan with their clipboards, questionnaires, and micro-cassette tape recorders, dead set on gathering enough information about this holy man to box him in, to define him properly to their bosses back home. And so the interrogation begins.

Question Number One: "Who are you?" Well, how would you answer that question? When I was in Guatemala several summers ago, our church group traveled one day to a nearby resort community near Lake Atitlan. On the way back our pickup truck was stopped, and we were questioned at some length by Guatemalan police officers. It took quite a bit of time to explain exactly who we were. I suppose it didn't help that we only had photocopies of our passports. I don't see anything suspicious in that, do you? They finally let us go after about a half-hour of questioning and eyebrow raising.

"Who are you?" was the first question from the Jordan River fact finding team. Might take a little while to answer that one, right? John's answer to the ecclesiastical police seems a bit strange to me at first. He says, *"I am not the Messiah."* Now I don't know about you, but if I was John in the wilderness wearing what he was wearing, that answer would not be on my short list. I think he should have opened with something a bit more innocuous like, "My father Zechariah was a priest and my mother's name was Elizabeth, and they lived in the Judean hill country not too far from here." But no, John chooses to raise a few eyebrows. "I am not the Messiah," he says. Did they *ask* if he was the Messiah? They did not. Policeman pulls me over for speeding. I've left my license at home. "Who are you?" asks the friendly officer. "I am not the Messiah," is my answer. Policeman writes that in his report and calls for backup assistance.

Question Number Two: "What then? Are you Elijah?" Let me tell you something. John looked a whale of a lot like Elijah. And the book of Malachi (4:5) clearly suggests that Elijah will return to precede the way for a Messiah. It was an honest mistake by the Jerusalem fact finders. But John's answer still frustrates them. "I am not." There's no box to check on their questionnaire. They're about ready to throw their ballpoint pens into the river. This was well before the days of Elvis impersonators and certainly nobody in their right mind went around as an Elijah impersonator. But the resemblance here was remarkable. I have some sympathy for the inquisitors.

So on to Question Number Three: "Are you the prophet?" John's answer is tantalizingly and frustratingly brief: "No." I like to think John gave them a little wink here.

By the time we get to Question Number Four, I think these interrogators have just about reached the limits of their patience. Even though the Bible cannot convey voice inflection, here's how I think the fourth question must have gone. *"Well, who the heck are you then, monkey man? Give us an answer for the bishops. What do you say about yourself that might fit into one of our boxes?"* But John's answer is just as slippery and evasive as the others. "I am the voice," he says. He's the *what*? "I am the voice." You think this didn't raise more eyebrows back in the city? "I am the voice of one crying out." He could not have raised any more consternation had he said something like, "I am the Artist Formerly Known as Prince."

It doesn't take long for Team Orthodox to ask the obvious. If you're counting, this is Question Number Five: "Why then, pray tell, are you baptizing if you have no credentials, no license to be doing such a thing? You didn't even go to seminary!"

And here the team from denominational headquarters learns who John really is. He is a witness. He is a testifier who washes and prepares. He is a voice. The narrator of this reading says it all: "John himself was not the light, but he came to testify to the light."

o   o   o

Who are you? How do you centrally define yourself? In terms of work? Blood kin? Money? Talents? Grades? What is the real core of your identity? How do you identify yourself to others? A recent article in *National Geographic*[10] describes the rise of Buddhism in the United States religious mainstream as people experiment with ancient meditation practices that are applied to a variety of situations ranging from addiction to incarceration to stress management. The appeal of Buddhism (catching on in North America with over three million practitioners in the U.S. and Canada) is an invitation to peel back pretense and artifice to reveal the core and authentic self created by God for specific and holy purpose. Counselors and therapists tell us that the number one challenge in patients they see surrounds this whole question of identity. So many of us never really come to know who it is we are. I'm reminded of Arthur Miller's classic drama, *Death of a Salesman*, where the family has gathered around the grave of Willy Loman. Willy's son, Biff, finally speaks the sad truth about his father: "He had the wrong dreams. . . . He never knew who he was."[11]

Maybe John the Baptist goes about it the right way out in the desert. He tells people who he is by first telling them *who he isn't*. "I am not the Messiah." What difference would it make if we reminded ourselves of that truth on a regular basis? Relatively few people claim out loud to be the Messiah, of course, although an emergency psychologist friend once told me that on a busy night several years ago he had three seriously ill patients in the same room after midnight and two of them were claiming to be Jesus. The two Jesus-es even got into an argument with each other. (The rest of us usually just don't notice or come clean that we're trying to serve as surrogate Messiahs in our own problems.)

Who hasn't tried to rescue a loved one from suffering only to discover that it's often impossible to protect someone from harm's way if they are bent on hurting themselves? What caring Christian has not tried to work for justice and peace in the world—to try and address and make a difference in a complex problem—only to discover that there are often dark and evil powers that perpetuate selfishness, greed, and violence, no matter how loving your witness might be? Who has not attempted to live life as their own personal Messiah, needing nobody else for counsel or community? Truth be told, we're probably all described in those questions to one degree or another.

∘ ∘ ∘

"Who are you?" the Jerusalem fact finders ask of John. But don't stop there. *Who are we?* We are people with definite limits.

There is a point any Christian reaches in their reflection and witness and disappointment where the most helpful thing to say is exactly what John said to his interrogators: "I am not the Messiah."

For those of us who've tried to be, there are few words as sweet.

For Reflection and Discussion

- *What difference would it make if we (with John) regularly confessed, "I am not the Messiah"?*

- *Why is individual identity such an important component of spiritual and emotional health?*

- *How do you describe yourself to someone you're just getting to know?*

Conception Consent

LUKE 1:26-38

I've come across a fair number of people in my pastoral career whose main stumbling block with Christianity is Mary's virgin birth. A woman once told me, "The story of the Virgin Mary is so extreme to me. Having a science background, I just can't accept this." The people who raise these concerns are faithful and thoughtful people who know about basic human anatomy and reproduction. And so when such a seemingly central part of the story cannot be explained, the whole thing quickly unravels for them.

It's never really been such a big problem for me that Mary conceived without a man's assistance. I suppose if God can create the giraffe, beluga whales, the color purple, and navel oranges, then a birth without the normal coupling of sperm and egg isn't such a stretch of the imagination.

But sometimes I wonder if Christians are not missing the whole point when we get stuck in these divine conception deliberations. I find it interesting that Mary's virginal state is mentioned three separate times in this story from Luke, once in the gospel of Matthew, and never again in the entire Bible. Mary is mentioned many times, of course, but her famous pregnancy, that is, the precise *modus operandi*, is only mentioned these four times. You'd expect to find many more. Search high and low and you won't.

It is theologically and intellectually fine with me that Jesus came into the world in this virginal fashion. I say the creed every Sunday with gusto and don't even flinch at the tough parts anymore. But I sometimes wonder if Mary's virginity doesn't overshadow the real miracle in the story. The thing that I find most fantastic and incredible is not *how* the Son of God finally wound up bellowing on barn straw, but *that* somebody like Mary chose to risk her reputation and say "yes" to it all. Mary said "okay" to God, "I'll do it." The operative word for me here is not *how* but rather *that*.

Philip Yancey tells a story about a young woman in his church in Chicago—an attorney, who stood bravely before their congregation one Sunday morning and confessed a sin that everyone knew about already. "We had seen her hyperactive son running up and down the aisles every Sunday," writes Yancey. "Cynthia had taken the lonely road of bearing an illegitimate child and caring for him after his father decided to skip town. Cynthia's sin was no worse than many others, and yet, as she told us, it had such conspicuous consequences. She could not hide the result of that single act of passion, sticking out as it did from her abdomen for months until a child emerged to change every hour of every day for the rest of her life. No wonder the Jewish teenager Mary felt greatly troubled: she faced the same prospects even without the act of passion."[12]

The thing that impresses me most in this story about the annunciation to Mary in Luke's gospel, occurring nine months prior to that first Christmas, is not *how* Jesus comes into the world but rather *that* Mary says "yes" to God's call. One morning she is happily dreaming about her upcoming wedding and life with Joseph, her fiancé.

The next day brings morning sickness and a story that will become increasingly difficult to explain to friends and family. Christmas cards often depict the bumpy road to Bethlehem as the lonely couple makes the arduous and dangerous journey from Nazareth. Heck, I'd say they were glad to get out of town given the months of whispering from the neighbors. So tell me. Which is the greater miracle here? The Virgin Birth or the Virgin's unmistakable *girth* after telling God, "Here am I"?

It can be a frightening thing to place oneself in the hands of God. To tell God, "Yes, here I am." I've absolutely no doubt that "the Lord is my shepherd," a consoling, comforting presence. Mary's own experience also teaches me that God's call is often not necessarily something one would personally choose if given that option. Her reaction to this call is not filled primarily with joy and happiness at first, but rather resignation and great fear. Mary was initially filled with perplexity and a ponderous spirit (1:29).

My son Lukas (who has given me permission to use this story) is never one to accept news without probing the cause. Upon learning of our move to a congregation in South Carolina, he kept boring into the purpose of leaving our home in Virginia, wanting with great intensity to know "Why? Why are we moving, Daddy?" I tried to explain to him something of God's call. His twelve-year-old reply must have been similar to Mary's first gut reaction, even though it's not printed in the scripture text. Lukas summed up the feelings of the whole family when he spoke with shades of the prophet Jeremiah, "WELL, IF GOD'S CALLING, TELL HIM TO SHUT UP, 'CAUSE I'M NOT LISTENING ANYMORE!!" If Mary didn't say that out loud, surely she thought it.

Mary eventually resigns herself to God's call when the angel says, "The power of the Most High will overshadow you." And of course we have read that text to symbolize how Mary will become miraculously pregnant by a divine agent. But I read the angelic promise differently these days. In this life we're given, it's always going to be a struggle between the will of the Most High and our own will. Inherent in any call will be this struggle to see who will "overshadow" the other, whose way will win out. C. S. Lewis said it well when he suggested that in the final analysis there are only two kinds of people. Those like Mary who say to God, "Thy will be done." And those people to whom God finally says, "*Thy* will be done." The angel said to Mary, "The Most High will overshadow you." The "you" in that sentence is important. To be overshadowed by God meant a demotion of what Mary wanted, what Mary was expecting for her life. It meant a scrambling of her future. To be "overshadowed" (this word will appear again with Peter, James, and John on the mountain of Transfiguration in Luke 9:34 as three disciples begin to discern that the way of Jesus does not jibe with their discipleship preferences) and relinquish the self for God's use must have brought on the morning sickness faster than the child who would soon grow inside her. I've personally wanted to vomit many times upon learning the consequences of a particular call.

What I'm trying to describe here—this fearful, overshadowing call of God—is not just for famous virgins. And it's not just for people who've happened to graduate from seminary. God's overshadowing call rests upon us all—all the baptized who have also been "ordained" with water and the word.

One of the authentic marks of this call is that we'll initially want to run the other way, retreating to safe ground and what has worked before, a truth amusingly illustrated by Jaroslav Pelikan in his book *Whose Bible Is It?*: "The language of the Bible can be like a set of dentist's instruments neatly laid out on a table, intriguing in their technological complexity and with their stainless steel highly polished—until they set to work on the job for which they were originally designed. Then all of a sudden my reaction changes from 'How shiny and beautiful they all are!' to 'Get that damned thing out of my mouth!'" (229). God will not let us linger very long with the sweetness and light of Christmas.

Let us all look to Mary for courage in our own calls from God, and look further beyond her pregnancy to the Savior who will help us answer. She was, after all, her son's first disciple. Even here, early on, she bears the cross. "Here am I," she says hopefully for us all. "Let it be with me according to your word."

For Reflection and Discussion

- *Why is our assent to God's call important? Why doesn't God just overpower our personal will in the matter?*

- *Describe a time in your life when you've been called upon to do something with risky implications.*

- *Read again the quote by Jaroslav Pelikan in this essay. What parts of the Bible are difficult for you to swallow?*

6

Marry a Pregnant Virgin

MATTHEW 1:18-25

A SIGNIFICANT PART OF any Protestant theological inheritance is derived from the brash witness of Martin Luther, a stubborn man who never backed down from a good argument—"Here I stand, I can do no other." I think that's a pretty clear summary of what the man was all about. Compromise is for wimps. It's important to know what we believe, unafraid to stand up for it. My wife insists I would argue with a maple tree if I thought there was any chance of changing its mind.

Once upon a time, a dedicated carpenter lived in the little burg of Nazareth. He was an honest and kind man, a righteous man, according to Matthew's version of the Christmas story. The word "righteousness" has fallen on hard times in our modern era. We usually use the word in a tone filled with contempt, as in the phrase "self-righteous." "Why *that Sally* is sure acting like a self-righteous prig today."

"Joseph was a *righteous* man." And that means he obeyed and upheld the Law—God's Law. He was an upstanding local citizen, engaged to his sweetheart, probably already saving a little nest egg from out of the sawdust, shavings, and sweepings of his shop. It's interesting that Joseph never says a word in any of the gospels. Like a stoic Scandinavian, he never once speaks. He was a serious man who always wanted to do the right thing. I'm guessing he was highly respected by the other citizens of his town as a solid man who knew what he believed and lived it out, not easily swayed by popular opinion.

So when Joseph hears that Mary is pregnant, well, you know what he's thinking. Joseph knows he's kept a tight rein on his own passions during this period of engagement. Safe sex in Joseph's day meant *no sex* until the "I do's." That can only mean one thing: Mary has been fooling around on the sly. You don't get pregnant by drinking the water, after all. Joseph is surely hurt and can't believe that Mary has been with some other guy. It's a simple judgment. The whole community will know the truth soon enough.

In the movie *Saved*, largely a parody about self-righteousness in the church, a young teenage girl named Mary becomes pregnant and the friends she once thought she had slowly vanish. She sits in church for the annual Christmas play and listens to the pastor read the traditional Christmas story about a virgin giving birth. Viewers overhear the Mary in the film think these thoughts to herself about the other famous Mary: "I know this is totally wrong," she thinks. "But don't you ever wonder if she made the whole thing up? I mean, you have to admit it's a good one. It's not like anyone could use Virgin Birth as an excuse again. I don't really think she made it up," Mary concludes, "but I sure can understand why a girl would."

Now don't forget this little detail. Joseph was a "righteous" man. He kept the Law, knew the Scriptures backwards and forwards. Joseph so much wants to do the right thing. He knew what God's word clearly said. According to the twenty-second chapter of Deuteronomy, it was fairly clear what the "right thing" to do was. It's right here in the Bible: "If there is a young woman, a virgin already engaged to be married, and a man meets her in the town and lies with her, you shall bring both of them to the gate of that town and stone them to death" (22:23-24). *The word of the Lord*. There it was in black and white. Joseph, being a righteous man, knew well the consequences of Mary's perceived misdeeds. The "right thing" was to follow the letter of the Law. It's right there in the Bible.

Here our story says that Joseph makes a decision. Joseph decides to spare Mary any "public disgrace," planning to dismiss her "quietly." Joseph could have dismissed her rather loudly but he doesn't. People are going to talk, but maybe this way she'll have some sort of chance at a new life.

That night Joseph has a strange dream. In a dream that goes against all reason, an angel says, "Fear not." Let me tell you a little secret. Whenever an angel says, "Don't be afraid" in the Bible, you can bet your bottom dollar that God is about to reveal a bit of news that will knock somebody's socks off. Joseph is asked to marry a pregnant virgin, something that went against all that Joseph understood or believed. But when Joseph woke up, he did that very thing— all without a word. He never once speaks, I'm telling you.

This version of the Christmas story, Matthew's version, is mainly about silent (but courageous) Joseph and how he chose to receive this new unplanned baby—Joseph, a normal guy living in a normal place working at a normal job who wanted to do the "right" thing, but wound up doing a new thing. The story is about someone who knew what *tradition* said to do (it was right there in black and white in the Bible), but was open instead to what *God* said to do. The story is about a faithful Judean who knew what he believed and was willing to argue about his beliefs with a maple tree, but instead took a chance and went in a new direction, guided by the Spirit.

Joseph's change of direction reminds me a lot of what Jesus would soon say in the Sermon on the Mount a bit later in this same book of Matthew (chapter 5): "You have heard that it was said to those of ancient times . . . *But I say to you* . . . You have heard that it was said, *but I say to you*." Over and again Jesus quotes a revered scriptural truth, then stands that truth on its head, giving us new teachings about love of enemies, avoiding vengeance, and alternatives to violence. Jesus could quote the scriptures with the best of them, but he was doing a new thing.

Sometimes the Bible can be used as a weapon against people. And maybe you have experienced the Bible in precisely this way—as a weapon. According to the Bible, Joseph had every right to dismiss Mary loudly, even violently. He had clear scriptural warrant. He was right. She was wrong. Or so it seemed. Joseph wanted to do the "right thing" and the scriptures gave him the green light to do so. He was a righteous man. Please don't forget this.

We who also want to do the "right thing" will consult scripture on a variety of issues ranging from capital punishment to human sexuality to divorce to the morality of war. And we will want to take a stand based on scripture, the word of God in black and white that we can quote and live by—a trustworthy source of inspiration for those who wish to do the right thing. "Here I stand, I can do no other." There are certain things I'm not going to budge about anytime soon. Same with you, I suspect.

The difficulty (and challenge) is that the Bible itself is often doing new things with issues we thought were long settled. The Bible fiddles around with things that seem to be set in stone and black and white. I was at a workshop once and heard the leader say a very strange thing. He said, "A sermon that begins in the Bible and ends in the Bible is not biblical." That's a rather odd but ultimately true statement. The Bible will always push us beyond its pages to the stuff of this life—unwanted pregnancies, ethical dilemmas, the radical nature of loving and forgiving those who have wronged us. The Bible is holy only to the extent that it intersects with the messiness and beauty of life. "The word is made flesh" *in us*—our flesh, our concrete and often messy lives.

Surprisingly, the real miracle of this Christmas story (as Matthew tells it) is not the Virgin Birth. Not really. (The amazing birth, I'll grant, is undeniably miraculous and I say so every time I confess the Apostles' Creed.) The real miracle, however, from my vantage point, is that a decent guy like Joseph (who lived a settled, holy life) could set out on a whole new path that contradicted all he'd ever known. The real miracle of this Christmas story is that quiet Joseph decided to listen to a living voice.

∘ ∘ ∘

So go ahead. *Marry a pregnant virgin* (even though scripture clearly forbids it).

Dare to stand by those who often feel shunned by the church. Reach out to those whom many claim the Bible clearly condemns. Speak up for those who suspect God's grace has passed them by.

This Christmas, in honor of the glorious birth, do a new thing.

For Reflection and Discussion

- *Think of someone you know like Joseph who does more than they say.*

- *How is the Bible occasionally used as a "weapon" against those who disagree?*

- *Reflect upon the statement, "A sermon that begins in the Bible and ends in the Bible is not biblical." Do you agree or disagree? Why?*

HE CHOSE US IN CHRIST BEFORE THE FOUNDATION OF THE

WORLD . . . DESTINED US FOR ADOPTION AS HIS CHILDREN.

(EPHESIANS 1:4-5)

Chosen, Destined, Marked

EPHESIANS 1:3-14

IN THE NOVEL *COLD Mountain*, there is a beautiful exchange between the two central female characters. Ruby has just arrived on a western North Carolina farm during the Civil War to help out Ada, who is something of a novice to mountain life. Ruby is trying to teach her new friend the rhythms of the land and asks Ada, as a test, why she thinks the sumac and the dogwood turn color in early fall in advance of the other trees, almost a full month ahead. "Chance?" replies Ada.

After noting that both trees are full of ripe berries in early fall, Ruby presses further. "What else is happening that might bear on the subject?" Birds were moving. "Enough to make you dizzy at the numbers of them." Ruby notes how "green and alike" all the trees must look to passing birds. "They don't know these woods. They don't know where a particular food might live." Ruby suggests that there is a design to early color change. "Dogwood and sumac maybe turn red to say *eat* to hungry stranger birds." Ada thinks on this information and says, "You seem to suppose that a dogwood might have a plan in this." "Well, maybe they do," says Ruby.[13]

It is usually near the beginning of the New Year that I think about large ideas such as destiny and divine design and the ever-elusive concept, "God's Plan for My Life." Am I really doing what God intends? Is my work in concert with God's will? Could I just as easily be a plumber (which has always intrigued me) or an elementary school teacher (which was my major in college)? This might alarm you that even pastors think about these things. After all, if *anybody* is supposed to clearly know what God has in mind for them, pastors should, right? The last time I played golf, somebody jokingly suggested the night before the game that it wouldn't rain the next day because (*ha-ha*) I had some divine connection to the weather. All in good fun, of course, but you get the picture. If anybody's got a direct pipeline to God, pastors are apparently the chosen ones.

But it's around this time of year that I play that very odd game that ultimately links me to only about two or three people from my past and a couple of seemingly innocuous turn-in-the-road events. Without these people and without those events, my life would be very different than it is today. If I hadn't gone to *this* college I would never have met *this* campus pastor or worked at *that* camp or majored in *that* discipline (which means that I would never have laid eyes on my wife Cindy and had these particular children or even gone to seminary at all). I would've been something else. And any of us here could reconstruct such a past where if you fiddled with one event *just a little bit*, or weren't in position to meet a person at just that right moment in time that one afternoon so long ago, then your whole life as you know it unravels—meaning it could have turned out very differently. Do you ever do this? Do you ever play this game? These little crossroads of the past link up with each other so seamlessly on paper, but take away any one of them. Tinker a bit with just a single afternoon from your past. And you're elsewhere, living another life.

Does God really have a specific plan for each of us? For each of the *six billion* people on the planet? Or do we career haphazardly from one choice and circumstance to another, for ill or good? Like the dogwood and sumac whose early color, year after year, guides traveling birds to food in the fall, is there also a divine design at work in our own lives, guiding us gently but insistently to the right place? These are important questions. Your answer reveals, to a very large extent, what you truly believe about God—how God consistently works (or maybe doesn't work) in the world.

Many modern people (including many Christians, if truth were told) believe that God created the world long ago, set it in motion, wound it up like a divine clockmaker, but then stepped back from the handiwork to let natural law unfold without divine interference. Such a theory has its advantages. For one, human freedom is honored and revered. For if God has a specific plan for each person, a course precisely decided upon and charted for each of us here on earth from the very get-go of conception, then how free are we truly to divert from such a course? And are we really willing to say, for example, that a mother on the brink of starvation in the Sudan due to local drought and famine is following God's intended path for her life? Or is she simply living out the consequences of her disobedience to that plan? I don't think we want to say either of those things. The theory of God as an ancient hands-off "clock winder" who releases dominion of the world to human resolve has a certain appeal for many thoughtful people. Does God have a plan? God indeed has a plan, according to this theory, but the plan is for a *world*, not individual lives.

According to the Bible, however, God is much more than a divine clock winder. In his beautiful letter to the Ephesians, Paul uses remarkably direct language in the first chapter about "God's plan" for the church. He uses words like *chosen* in verse 4: "God chose us in Christ before the foundation of the world." Please note that we are chosen, according to Paul, not after we've earned it or somehow measured up. A person is chosen for promotion based on work well done. A kid is chosen first for a pick-up softball game because she can hit well. Any child waiting alone at second base, sheepishly kicking the dust after everyone else has been selected, learns this lesson early. We are usually chosen on the basis of ability or performance. Paul says that God chose us before the very foundations of the world came into being. We're talking here about *pre-Jurassic selection*. It almost sounds like an arranged marriage. Our freedom in the matter seems to be in jeopardy. Am I reading this correctly? Before the world came into being, before sperm found egg, God, according to Paul, had you and me clearly in mind. It's a lot to digest all at once.

And not only are we chosen, Paul also asserts that we are *destined* in verses 5 and 11. Destined for adoption. Destiny: divine choice with purpose and intention. Destined to be a teacher? A doctor? A househusband? An accountant? A retiree? A student? A plumber? A preacher, God forbid? Destined? The word carries so much drama, so much standing-on-the-cliff-with-the-wind-blowing-through-your-hair theatrics, shouting, "*THIS?!! Is this what you want me to do, O Lord? Is this what you had in mind?*" Destiny. It's a word we don't use much anymore. It's easier to believe we have stumbled into a profession, come upon a vocation by luck or chance.

And to top it all off, Paul asserts in verse 13 that we were *marked* by the Holy Spirit. Chosen, destined, marked. These are not verbs that describe a relationship with an impersonal, clock-winding God. These are verbs that describe an active, imaginative, creative God who has designs and claims on our lives—a God who intimately and lovingly had us in mind from the beginning.

When my younger brother Lee was in his formative years, dabbling with the likes of Nietzsche and Karl Marx and Malcolm X, rejecting for the most part God, church, and Jesus, my mother used to take great comfort from that line in the Lutheran baptismal liturgy that makes this bold claim: "Child of God, you have been sealed with the Holy Spirit and marked with the cross of Christ forever."

Marked. Branded. Chosen. Forever. My mom took great comfort in that line; she even smiled broadly in church whenever the words were invoked, squeezed my father's knee, and knowingly patted the empty seat once warmed by her son. For God's presence in his life, you see, was not up to her (or even up to my brother). It was completely out of her hands. Instead, her son's destiny was in the lap of God who "chose us before the foundation of the world." Marked. Chosen. She slept peacefully, most of the time anyway.

Do we have freedom in this choosing, this destiny, this branding? Of course. We can and do reject the path God has in mind for us. Frederick Buechner, author and theologian, has written wise words for us all: "There are all kinds of voices calling you to all different kinds of work, and the problem is to find out which is the voice of God rather than of Society, say, or the Superego, or Self-Interest." Buechner goes on to share this important point: "The place God calls you to is the place where your deep gladness and the world's deep hunger meet."[14]

Vocation and calling are vitally important elements of what Christmas is all about. Not just that Christ was born and fulfilled *his* chosen destiny. But also that we are born and fulfill *ours*. The word became flesh and lived among us, says John in his gospel. But that same Word becomes flesh and lives in us. That too is gospel.

Each person plays an important part in God's plan. You have been chosen. You have been destined. You have been marked. In this New Year, think about the turns in the road from your past. Like the dogwood and sumac, they are placed before us for a reason, by more than random chance. Discovering that reason is a large part of what it means to believe.

For Reflection and Discussion

- *Do you believe that God has a plan for each of the six billion people on the planet? Why or why not?*

- *Read again the lesson from Ephesians 1:3-14 and note the verbs—chosen, destined, and marked. Now look back on your life and choose one or two incidents, perhaps "chance" encounters, without which your life would be completely different.*

- *How are you beginning to understand the biblical concept of a "call" from God?*

EPIPHANY

Epiphany

epiphany: an appearance or manifestation, especially of a divine being

The Epiphany season always begins with a star, leads to a river, and ends on a mountain—the nocturnal journey of the magi, Jesus' baptismal dip, and three disciples' peek from a peak. It strikes me that not a single epiphany occurs indoors.

The Bible teaches us that God is revealed through an abundance of natural phenomena. With Elijah God goes spelunking, comforting the poor guy in a cave as he flees the wrath of Jezebel. A monsoon is a sign of God's revelation for Noah. Ruth senses God's guidance while gleaning in the fields. Zacchaeus begins his relationship with Jesus from the top of tree. A dry, lifeless desert of bones becomes a symbol for Ezekiel that God will restore his people and breathe new life into them. John of Patmos sees a hopeful vision for a persecuted church while exiled on an island. Stephen, who was stoned not long after the birth of the church, once confessed: "The Most High does not dwell in houses made with human hands" (Acts 7:48). I suspect there is a connection between this statement and his death at the hands of angry religious leaders.

God, of course, regularly shows up in church buildings, and liturgical epiphanies experienced therein certainly help us to recognize God elsewhere. But we cannot limit or corner God. Someone once said, "Don't try slapping God on the back. You'll miss." God's presence completely fills the universe. "Where can I go from your Spirit?" asks the psalmist. "Or where can I flee from your presence?" (Psalm 139:7). The implied answer to both questions is that God permeates an entire cosmos and beyond.

We are a worshipping people who gather weekly for comfort, sustenance, and good news in houses built of stone and wood. We are people of font and table. We sing and are sent in a rhythm that has become normative and healing for millions. What we might learn during Epiphany is that this old liturgical pattern is delightfully portable. Paying attention to its old truths, the liturgy reveals the myriad epiphanies occurring in God's created order, just outside our back doors.

". . . and there, ahead of them, went the star that they had seen at its rising, until it stopped over the place where the child was." (Matthew 2:9)

The Latecomers

once upon a time three men set out upon a long journey. I say "three," although we really don't know their number. Could've been more, I suppose, or less. Nor do we know their names. You might mentally file away that part of the tale. Maybe you can locate your own story in theirs somehow.

MATTHEW 2:1-12

Well, anyway, these three guys start out, and you have to wonder why. They were magi, after all, and although we're not really sure what such people did, whether they were magicians or astrologers or just what, they were from the "East"—the exotic land of mystery and wealth. And we know they had pretty expensive gifts in their saddlebags. They could rack up a pretty hefty credit balance on their Persian National Bank Visa Card, and everyone knew they were good for it. They were undoubtedly well-educated types who had access to the best wisdom and learning money could buy, matriculating at some Ivy League school of the East with high honors.

And so that's curious to me: why they started out at all. Why these smart, rich, wise guys bother to board camels and follow a star. Didn't they have everything they needed back East? Maybe something was missing in their lives, as is often true in our own American culture. Sometimes those with the most education, most opportunities, and most money are strangely among the emptiest and saddest of people. I have no idea whether this is true of our three friends, but it just seems strange to me that they would start out at all on such a journey. What was it about their lives that made them leave all that they had and set out into the great unknown? Something must have been missing for these three nameless sages who followed a star.

Their journey leads them to Jerusalem, and they seem to have no trouble getting in to see King Herod, which again says something about the connections and clout of our three friends. Herod is lounging there on his throne, surrounded by guards, fawning women and luxury. The magi ask only one simple question. "Where is the child who has been born king of the Jews?" Herod almost chokes on his goat cheese. He thinks to himself, *Wait a minute, I thought I was King of the Jews.* Herod, of course, was a Roman ruler but was given jurisdiction over the Jews in this corner of the Empire. This little question offered by the visitors from the East so unnerves and frightens Herod that his Royal Highness has to excuse himself.

The local ministerial association is called together, the keepers of biblical truth, and Herod tosses a question their way. His eyes are like those of a cornered deer. "Where is the Messiah supposed to be born?" You get the distinct impression that they'd better give the right answer. The clergymen sweat buckets and scroll through their concordances and finally come upon an obscure reference from the fifth chapter of the Book of Micah. "In Bethlehem, your highness, nine miles away." This news shocks the king as much as anybody. Messiahs aren't usually born in out-of-the-way Podunks.

Herod quickly calls for a secret meeting of the magi who have been receiving massages from the royal masseuse. (It doesn't really say that, but try riding on a camel for a couple of weeks and see if you don't need one.) The magi are then given a royal assignment that a second-grader can see right through a mile away, but which is received as genuine and heartfelt by our travelers at the time. "Go down the road nine miles and search for this child," instructs Herod. "When you find him send word back to me. I'd really like to worship him, too." Right, Mr. Goat Cheese Breath. Herod, this man with enormous power, seems unduly threatened by somebody wearing diapers.

Now don't get too sidetracked by the star that leads our three friends along, this moving celestial body with a mind of its own. Some think it was Halley's Comet before there was a Halley to name it. But it doesn't really matter what it was. The presence of a guiding star simply serves as another dramatic contrast in the story. The real power in the world isn't in the wealth of Persia or in the grandeur of Herod's courts. The real power in the world is beyond human control. You get the feeling that these magi are learning a good bit about wonder and awe well before they reach Bethlehem.

And so the nine miles go by quickly that night. Our friends locate Jesus and his parents. Curiously, the holy family is now in a "house" (Matthew 2:11), not a manger or a barn or a cave, which means that some time has elapsed since the actual birth. The baby Jesus has moved to different accommodations. The magi, then, are latecomers to Bethlehem, arriving long after the angels have returned to heaven and the shepherds have gone back to their jobs. You might mentally file away that little detail as well. They were late. (Maybe these travelers are symbolic of so many of us who come to Jesus later in life.)

And so our friends duck into the house, kneeling before the child. It's immediately obvious that the gifts they unpack are ludicrously mismatched for a baby. They see right away, even if they are men, that maybe a blanket, a rattle, and a board book would have been better choices. They kneel and open their treasure chests and lay these impractical, expensive gifts at the feet of the baby. Myrrh seems to be a particularly odd choice, a resin used for anointing and embalming a corpse. "Happy Birthday, little boy, here's a little something for your death." But we're getting ahead of the story, aren't we?

In a dream the magi are warned not to return to Herod. They return home by another road. (James Taylor, by the way, recorded a marvelous song several years ago depicting the new road taken by the magi. It's called *Home by Another Way*, if you're interested.) It's been a long, strange journey for these three: these nameless, wealthy, educated wise ones who are latecomers to Bethlehem and who take another way home.

Well, if you haven't guessed where I'm going with this, I'll just say it. This story near the very beginning of Matthew's gospel is our story—we, the wealthy and educated and wise of the world who hail from the most powerful country on the planet. It will take us a little longer to come to Jesus, to even sense that we need Jesus when so much else is out there to save us and vie for our attention. And even when we do sense the need, it will mean a long, circuitous trip with many starts and stops. Ours is a culture in which we often painfully straddle the kingdom of Herod and the kingdom of Jesus, with one foot in either place: the kingdom of power versus the kingdom of sacrifice. Both will tug on us mightily. And living as we do, where we do, it is sometimes anybody's best guess which kingdom has me (and you) most in its thrall.

They were wealthy, educated, and powerful, these three who came to Jesus. I sometimes wonder why in the world they needed to make the trip—what was missing in their lives exactly. It would seem they had everything already-everything one might need.

One sure sign, I think, that these three truly found what they were looking for was not the miraculous star. One sure sign that they had found what was missing in their lives is that they went home by another road. They chose Jesus over Herod.

Not much has changed for those who straddle two worlds since that starry night so long ago. Sometimes the road before us is just that clear.

For Reflection and Discussion

- *Perhaps you are someone who has come searching for Jesus as a "latecomer." What has caused you to start out on this journey?*

- *Why do you think that Herod, one of the most powerful men on earth, is so unnerved by the birth of this small baby?*

- *Locate a recording of James Taylor's song, "Home by Another Way." Listen to the song several times and note your reactions.*

2

Gospel Imperative

MARK 1:4-11

GO DO YOUR HOMEWORK. Take out the trash. Have that on my desk by 4:00. Write your thank-you notes. Make your bed. Call your mother. Run by the grocery store for some milk. Sweep the sidewalk. Feed the dog. Wash the dishes. Say you're sorry. Brush your teeth. Get out and vote. Balance the checkbook. Support the troops. Stand for Hymn #557. Slow down, reduced speed ahead. Read your Bible. Buy something.

Do you know what all those phrases have in common? They all begin with an *imperative* verb. They direct us to do something right away. Imperative verbs often carry with them a sense of compelling urgency. Our lives are so laden with imperative verbs that we hardly notice how many compete for our attention. Urgent, often strident, commands assemble every single day before the morning is even an hour old. Admittedly, there is a certain security and safety in being told by an authoritative voice what to do and when.

Without some imperative verbs, of course, there would be chaos. When someone is about ready to step off a curb in front of a rapidly moving taxicab, we don't say, "Pardon me, sir, but there is a speedy yellow vehicle moving into your ambulatory path." We say, *"Look out!"* Martin Luther King Jr., could not tell a nation something like, "Well, I know you've got other things on your mind these days, other things to think about and all, but would you please, pretty please, consider the injustice of racism maybe when you get around to it?" His message was direct and urgent: "Repent, for we have sinned as a nation." We need the imperative to warn, correct, and guide. Even so, it's easy to become so immersed in this imperative life that one can miss how driven we are by verbs that always direct us to some sort of action.

As Jesus stands in the river in Mark's gospel, dripping wet from his baptism, a voice from heaven speaks. I've often wondered about this divine voice. You'd think an imperative tone would be in order. "All right Jesus, you've been dunked and commissioned, now get out there and save the world. Feed the poor. Befriend the lonely. Hang on a cross for the whole human race." But there's not a single imperative verb here. No instructions, no fatherly advice, no pep talk leading to action. Instead, we hear this: "You are my Son, the beloved; with you I am well pleased."

I find these words to be among the most remarkable in all of the gospels. At this baptism, God declares two essential things: (1) how much Jesus is loved and (2) how much God is pleased by Jesus. In our achievement-centered, goal-assessed, imperative verb-driven world, I am left wondering exactly *how* Jesus pleases God. He has done absolutely nothing of note so far in this gospel—no healings, no good deeds, no snazzy teachings: zippo. Jesus just stands there in the water, and God declares his undying love and pleasure.

So tell me. God declares his love on the basis of—*what?* Apparently, on the basis of grace. When it comes to love, the indicative always precedes the imperative. "You *are* my Son," says God. Never once does God say, "Since you're my Son, you really oughta be doing such and such." Never once does God say, "After all I've done for you . . ."

I suspect deep down that this clear announcement of his unconditional identity is the very thing that allowed Jesus to live the way he did—sacrificially and for others. All too often our lives are played out in shame and guilt and how we fail to measure up to someone's expectations, another's perceptions of our inadequacies. Imperatives litter our lives, and we know we ought to change. But somehow these admonitions lack very little power in getting to the heart of what truly ails us. Why are we so quick to admonish and correct, and so slow to bless and affirm?

Jesus stood in the water, and the voice spoke only of divine pleasure. Could the same be true of every baptism—that every time water is poured in Jesus' name, we are given the same core identity? "You *are* my child, the Beloved; with *you* I am well pleased." Think about that for a moment. Heck, think about it for a lifetime. Think about living from such a gospel identity before we do a blessed thing to try and please God—his pleasure in us exponentially outweighing our feeble attempts to try and please him. Jesus heard that voice and concluded that he could serve such a God, even die for such a God. I'm convinced that people cannot be goaded into change. We can, however, be loved into it.

o   o   o

I read a story a while back of a woman named Kristen who would give money to a homeless woman named Ann on her way to worship each Sunday. I'm sure that Kristen knew all the reasons for not doing that, but she did it anyway. Kristen was out of town for a few weeks and when she returned, Ann excitedly hobbled up to greet her, gave Kristen a hug, and wondered whether she had been sick. After worship, Kristen invited this homeless woman to her home for lunch. It turned out that Ann was once a centrifuge specialist in a local hospital until contracting rheumatoid arthritis. Her disability payments did not cover her rent, so she lived in a car. The two women began a long friendship at lunch that day. Kristen learned something about her friendship with this old forgotten woman. "Being generous to

the poor," said Kristen, "means being present to them and knowing them."

So often when I go to help someone, in whatever sad situation
it might be, I try to think of ways to help the person cope or maybe
"change for the best." What this usually means is that I intend to
maintain my emotional distance and not get overly involved—boundary issues and all that. Pastors like me thrive on calendars, appointments, brief visits filled with short snippets of Christian advice.
What people need most, however, is what Kristen was able to give
this homeless woman, her new friend. It's the same thing that Jesus
received in the water that day—beloved companionship and unconditional pleasure in the friendship. "With you I am well pleased."
Nothing expected in return—just pure and simple grace.

I am well aware that many people face situations where "tough
love" is called for in a relationship with a child, spouse, friend, or
family member. Even there, however, the creative *announcement* of
this grace, our core liquid identity in baptism, is our shared calling—even in the midst of tough consequences for those we love.

o o o

For many years, on the Feast of Saint John, the third day of Christmas, I've hiked to the top of Table Rock in upstate South Carolina,
not far from the home of my wife's parents. This past December 27, I
parked the car at the trailhead at first light and started up the mountain alone, about four miles, one way, to the summit at 3100 feet. It
was a fine clear morning. The stream beside one stretch of the trail
made wonderful noises. I passed two young women from a nearby
college on the way up and then had the mountain all to myself.

Table Rock's big smooth rock face can be seen from miles away. I
sat at the top of that rock face for some time and took in a sweeping
vista that included Caesar's Head, the Greenville city reservoir, and
the city of Greenville itself. Facing East and South, I even imagined
Columbia, my home, way off in the distance and the tall spire of our
church building in the heart of the city; these sights, of course, too
far away to actually view.

I pulled out my pocket New Testament and read aloud into the wind, words to commemorate Saint John: "In the beginning was the Word, and the Word was with God, and the Word was God. He was in the beginning with God. *All things came into being through him*, and without him not one thing came into being" (John 1:1-3). Not a single thing, not a single self-made person.

Mountains are holy, I think, in the Bible, in Native American tradition, in the hearts of all who need a long view, because they give us perspective—perspective on a life, my life and yours, here only for a short while compared to the grand sweep of geologic time.

Long ago, out of that long view of time and space, a voice spoke over the waters—an old, creative voice of affirmation. "You are my Son, the beloved; with you I am well pleased."

Listen for that voice in your own life—it will make all the difference in your long and glorious view of this world. The indicative trumps the imperative every time.

"You *are* my child, the beloved."

You are.

For Reflection and Discussion

- *Try to make a list of the imperative commands you've either heard or used today.*

- *Think of a time in your life when someone loved you unconditionally, even though you'd done nothing to deserve it. What difference did that love make in your life?*

- *What would happen in our congregations if we tried to hear God's words to Jesus in the Jordan also spoken at the baptism of every child or adult?*

His Hem

ISAIAH 6:1-13

In the year that King Uzziah died, 742 BC, two and three quarter millennia ago, the soon-to-be prophet Isaiah was sitting in the temple minding his own business, worshipping God in liturgical routine. It may surprise you to know that Isaiah was married and had children. He was a husband and a dad—a fairly normal life. That morning dawned like many other Sabbath mornings—some hymns, some holy words, and home.

But suddenly, Isaiah saw the Lord perched high above him on a throne, not to mention strange creatures with six wings, a miniature earthquake, and smoke that rivaled the fireworks of the great and powerful Oz. I can't pretend to know what all of this means. I've yet to meet your standard *dual-winged* angel, never mind a seraph. If you ask me, this sounds a bit like the opium-induced poetry of

Samuel Taylor Coleridge, who wrote that weird *Kubla Khan* we were forced to read in high school. Trains rumble through my city and perhaps shake "the pivots on the thresholds" of our church building from time to time, but never from anyone's voice. The congregation I serve is filled with quiet, subdued people not known for much religious emotion.

This vision from Isaiah is rather bizarre for most reserved church people. For example, if a pastor came at you during communion one Sunday morning not with bread and wine, but rather a pair of metal tongs and a hot glowing coal from the altar and tried to touch your lips with that—well, that would about do it for most liturgical people used to an expected routine. Average attendance would plummet. People might call the bishop. "*It's not in the bulletin*," we'd say. Isaiah's vision makes us a little nervous—so spontaneous and unplanned. But hey, it happened once; it could happen again. So buckle your Sunday safety belts.

Out of all the rich details in this story of Isaiah's call, one grabs my attention more than any other. Isaiah reports that the *hem*, just the tip of God's robe, absolutely filled the temple (which was no small place). Just the edge of his alb washed over the people like waves. Just a *sliver* of God's slip completely covers what had taken Jerusalem Carpet World months to match. Isaiah was face-to-face with grandeur and awe: feelings you get when looking at the Grand Canyon, or a sunrise at the beach, or even Seven States from Rock City—ultimate, large feelings that remind us how small we really are in relation to the vastness of God's universe.

Isaiah reports that this vision literally scared the hell out of him. "Woe is me! I am lost." Isaiah saw the fullness of God, which was frankly a mortal danger according to the Old Testament. If you happened to catch even a glimpse of God, well, it was curtains for you. One could not casually look at God and live. Moses wore a veil, you might remember, in his chatty wilderness conversations with God, but Isaiah saw everything. He rightly confesses, "I am lost . . . my eyes have seen the king!" And a whole lot more. Knowing the consequences of viewing the full-frontal God drove Isaiah to his knees.

Isaiah surely swoons from what he sees, but it may be that he faints dead away from what he hears. The seraphs are singing an amazing song. It's the same song we sing every week in the liturgy just before Holy Communion. "Holy, holy, holy, the whole earth is full of God's glory." Just as the temple is filled with God's hem, so too is the earth filled with God's glory. God fills the earth like God fills the temple. Same word, same image, only a verse apart.

The whole earth is full of God. The earth is sated with God's presence. There is perhaps no more important statement of ecological affirmation in the entire Bible. The holiness of God is in all things. God is in all places. The earth is spilling over with the divine.

Do you see why Isaiah hits his knees? As long as God could be kept corralled in the temple in liturgical routine, then God could be managed, tolerated, and watched. It was only an hour a week, after all. God could be kept on the margins of Isaiah's life, at a safe distance. But what he saw and heard changed everything that day. The light bulb in our boy's head was timed with his confession. "If God's hem fills this huge place," he thought, "then the rest of God's robe is spilling into my tomorrow, my week, my whole life." The jig was up for Isaiah. "Woe is me!" There was no place now to hide, no place in his week where God wasn't.

We church people are in dire need of a conversion like Isaiah's. I doubt we'll ever experience some Sunday morning the drama equaling this vision from 742 BC. But who am I to say that? I can say for sure that I stand in need of a conversion like Isaiah's. The most curious oxymoron in our common church vocabulary is the unfortunate phrase "worship hour." The worship *hour*. It happens every Sunday morning in sanctuaries across the country as people gather with scrubbed faces and best behavior to honor and praise God. It's tempting to point only to a certain day and hour when we think about encountering God. The seraphs put an end to that fallacy. "The whole earth is full of God's glory." Altars abound. One of the primary purposes of Sunday morning is to teach us where to look for God throughout the week.

A wonderful case study of Isaiah's conversion experience is

conveniently repeated for us in the call of the first disciples (Luke 5:1-11). Peter and friends have been fishing all night with no luck and up walks Jesus who teaches a while from an empty boat. No fish. Not a guppy. Jesus instructs Peter to try his luck again. And you know the result. But notice verse 7. "So they signaled their partners in the other boat to come and help them. And they came and filled both boats, so that they began to sink." *Filled*. Recall the same word from Isaiah's vision. Peter hits his knees. Is he afraid of drowning? Just like Isaiah, Peter suddenly knows the jig is up: no place exists where God *isn't*. No longer could Peter manage God. So he kneels right there in the middle of a workday, right there among the flopping flounder. It's a strange place for an altar. Peter's day job, as he once knew it, is over.

"Woe is me," said Isaiah. "Go away from me, Lord," said Peter. Knowing that "the whole earth" is full of God may be bad news at first for people like us who want to keep certain aspects of our lives separate, private, and self-sufficient. But in truth, this old song is the very best news anyone could possibly hear. "Holy, holy, holy, God fills the whole earth." What a gift we've been given by a God whose "hem" fills our worship spaces and spills over into all our times and places.

This is a great need for the church in a new century: that we begin to see the patterns offered in the Sunday liturgy as the pattern for our daily lives. When we come into contact with water in its manifold occurrences, ranging from the kitchen sink to the rapids of your local river, is not this a time to remember our common baptism and give thanks? When we prepare and eat food in all of its astonishing variety, is not this a time to recall the banquet of grace, offer thanks for God's constant communion in our lives, and remember the hungry in our midst? Even when we do something as mundane as taking out the garbage, is not this a moment to recall those we may have treated like garbage (near or far), confess our sin to them, and ask for forgiveness?

Believing that the world is infused with God, saturated with holiness, makes a huge difference in how we live, in how we treat people within and beyond our worship spaces, in how we honor and care for the earth, and in how we approach even the most predictable of activities.

His *hem*. That's what Isaiah saw. And that's what we see in worship—just a foretaste, a holy sliver, of what is coming and fills the world each day.

Holy, holy, holy. The whole earth full. In the most unlikely of places: watch.

Altars abound. So where shall we not kneel?

For Reflection and Discussion

- *Try to envision worship not as a segregated hour, but rather as a repeated pattern meant to connect with daily life. What part of the liturgy is most meaningful to you? Why?*

- *Reflect upon the many ways we tend to try and manage God within a defined worship space. If just the "hem" of God's robe fills the temple in Isaiah's vision, how does that suggest change in how we now live?*

- *Try making sacramental connections between Baptism and Holy Communion any time you encounter water or food in the coming week.*

4

Jesus Is the Question

JOHN 1:35-42

I WAS IN BELK'S DEPARTMENT Store at our local mall just before Christmas, looking for a gift for Cindy, my wife. I knew exactly what I wanted, what she wanted— a Clinique fragrance known as "Happy." I am not a mall sort of guy. My plan was to make a beeline for the cosmetics department, get what I needed, and get out. I always shop this way, with single-minded purpose. Blue-light specials and once-in-a-lifetime bargains do not sway me, and they fall on deaf ears. If you desire a companion with whom to browse leisurely and chattily in a shopping center, I am not your man.

Smart store managers, I'm convinced, station certain personnel in strategic locations watching for people like me—the lost and disoriented, wandering in a fog of choices. The attendant's question that day was intended to help narrow the field, but I took it as highly theological and suggestive: "Well, what are you looking for?" said the friendly Belk's attendant. I must have appeared certifiably dazed and confused, so she repeated it: *May I help you? What are you looking for?*

There are a lot of great questions in the Bible. I've always loved that moment in Genesis, just after the forbidden fruit incident, where God strolls through the Garden and coyly asks, "Where are you?" God knew where the man and woman were—hiding and ashamed, full of guilt. But the question also rings across the ages and addresses us, existentially, now, in the present. *Where are you? Where am I?* Where indeed? It can be a rather disorienting question if you think about it hard enough. God, I'm guessing, intends that.

"May I help you?" she asked. *What are you looking for?* Now there's a question to ponder. She meant it one way. I took it another way. Had she not had the appearance of someone ready to press the silent alarm button, I might still be staring at her, glassy-eyed. *What are you looking for?*

о   о   о

Some prospective disciples approach Jesus in the early scenes of John's gospel. The Lord is walking by, out for a morning stroll I guess, and John the Baptist points excitedly and says, "There he goes, that guy right there. He's the one I've been talking about, the Lamb of God." Two of John's disciples decide to follow, Andrew and a companion who remains un-named. Now why do you think one of them is un-named? Is the author of this gospel making room for you and me here? (Knowing how John's gospel works in multiple meanings, piling layer upon layer, a virtual sea of metaphors by the end of the book, I'd say maybe so.)

The two catch up to Jesus. But before they catch him, the story says that Jesus "turned and saw them following." Here's a little Bible tip for you. Jesus is on the road quite a bit in the gospels, and fairly often, he stops in the middle of the road, turns, and says something. Now watch for this; watch for the slow turn and watch what he then says. The "turn" always suggests a turn in the lives of those who follow—some important sign up ahead. "There's the guy," says John the

Baptist. "He's the one." And so off they go, Andrew and another un-named disciple. Let's pretend it's you.

And so Jesus turns and says, *"What are you looking for?"* By the way, these are the very first words spoken by Jesus in the gospel of John, the very first words out of his mouth. It's no accident that toward the end of this gospel, Jesus addresses the soldiers who come to arrest him with a similar question: *"Whom are you looking for?"* (18:4).

Please don't miss this. Jesus turns on that road and he could have said any number of things to these two who follow and want to know more about him. Jesus could have said, "Hey, I'm the son of God, the heavenly cat's meow, the right-hand man, the theological golden boy." Jesus could have made any number of theological assertions about himself, about God, about requirements of being his disciple. He had their attention. Why not cut to the chase and go straight for the doctrinal jugular? It's a perfect opportunity to offer theological clarity. But listen: Jesus' first words are a question. *What are you look-ing for?*

o o o

Many of our attempts at evangelism fail because we do not begin where Jesus began. When I encounter someone outside the church who seems interested in Christianity, I often attempt to say far too much in too little time because I fear this meeting may be the last. But look at this story. Notice, for example, that Jesus does not try to foist an orthodox explanation of the Apostles' Creed on these two guys. He cites no Bible verses, hands out no religious tracts, and twists nobody's arm. Jesus asks a single question and offers a short invitation, "Come and see." There is certainly a time for doctrinal clarity. There is much to be said for sound teaching and orthodox theology. But Jesus does not begin there. He begins with a single question: *What are you looking for?*

This is not only an important question to pose to people first coming to Jesus. It's also an important question for people who've been part of the church for years. Sometimes I think we reach a point in our faith development where we stop asking good questions, stop looking. Our faith becomes a series of settled assertions about Jesus and God that need no further perusal or examination. I remember in elementary school how it was important to know a series of facts and regurgitate those facts to please the teacher. *Who was the 32nd President of the United States?* I suppose it's important to know the correct answer is Franklin Delano Roosevelt, but even more important is the question: *What made FDR a great President? What are you looking for in a great President?*

In a similar way, it's easy to get stuck in the "correct" facts of faith and stop thinking about God in the here and now. Jesus, please note, never turns to the two followers on the road and asks, "What are you looking *at?*" The church is often quite adept at looking at Jesus, tallying facts about his life and admiring his wise teachings. *True or False: Jesus walked on water. True or False: He fed five thousand. True or False: Jesus once told a story about a Samaritan.* It's easy to get stuck in the facts and never go further and look for the meaning in these stories or in the church habits we take for granted. From the get-go, Jesus wants to know: *What are you looking for?* He assumes that faith involves a search, a journey—never an arrival, a settled destination. And he's asking where you are on that journey.

In the Epiphany season the church remembers the witness of Dr. Martin Luther King Jr. It's important to remember that the civil rights movement was essentially about helping people see that Jesus is alive in the world and that faith in him is never static, never completely settled and nailed down. Following Jesus always means that our most treasured beliefs and intentions are regularly examined, worthy of reflection and even revision. *What are you looking for?* Dr. King was many things for this nation, but he was primarily a Christian who never stopped looking.

I often see a bumper sticker that says, "Jesus Is the Answer," and I believe that assertion with all my heart. But I do not believe that's the place to begin with non-Christian people or even with ourselves. According to this old story, Jesus is actually the question. He invites us to ponder, wonder, search, and scratch our heads. And until we do that, I fear that we'll be looking *at* Jesus rather than *for* him. Perhaps that's a small distinction for you, but it actually has made all the difference in the world in my own life. I'm convinced there is a built-in tendency in all of us to search for meaning and truth. But be careful. It's easy to replace truth with a string of facts.

o   o   o

Toward the end of this story, Andrew excitedly runs to "first" find his brother Peter and let him in on the news. John reports that it "was about four o'clock in the afternoon." I've always loved that detail. *Four o'clock in the afternoon*. This is how authentic evangelism works. When we encounter the living Jesus (not the Jesus of historical facts), we will run and tell others. Every day our every o'clock will be filled with Jesus and his gospel intersecting with all the hours we are given. We run in haste to share.

You might want to begin the conversation something like this— *What are you looking for?*

For Reflection and Discussion

- *Assuming that you may be new to the Bible and church life, respond to Jesus' question that serves as the centerpiece of this essay.*

- *Name and describe two of your favorite teachers. Why were they effective? What sort of questions did they ask?*

- *Consult a mature Christian friend and ask them to make a list of their favorite questions in the Bible and why these questions pique their interest.*

5

Getting Ticked at Jesus

IN THE 1960S, BAPTIST
minister Will Campbell
was a key player in the civil
rights movement. He was
jailed, his life was threatened, and his children were

LUKE 4:14-30

ridiculed. All of that. But Will once
did a rather odd thing. He decided to
infiltrate a meeting of the Ku Klux Klan with
the intent of befriending several local Klan members. He said that
the oppressors needed to hear about the teachings and love of Jesus
as much or more than the oppressed. Now how do you think that went
over with Will Campbell's friends who were working for racial justice in the civil rights movement? You're right. They didn't like it.[15]

Sister Helen Prejean, author of the book *Dead Man Walking*, is a
Roman Catholic nun who has spent much of her ministry in pris-
ons with inmates, particularly death-row inmates. Family members
in her local congregation once lost their daughter in a brutal rape

and murder that shook the entire community for months. Then Sister Helen did a rather odd thing. She started visiting the man in her prison who had committed the crime. How do you think that went over with the parents of the young woman who had been brutally killed? You're right. They didn't like it.

I once knew two couples who were fast friends for many years. They went everywhere together including vacation trips and holidays. One of the marriages dissolved when the wife had an affair with a co-worker. The other couple then did a rather odd thing. They did not condone the behavior that broke up the marriage but tried to remain in touch with both friends. Now how do you think that went over with the husband whose wife betrayed him? You're right. He didn't like it.

In any community there are people whom we cannot stand. People we would not think of sitting next to. That's as true of the general population as it is of a particular congregational community. Our lists might differ, but we all draw the line somewhere. *Somebody* coming through the church doors might make us uncomfortable to be around—a family member we no longer speak to, an ex-spouse, a former friend, a homeless stranger who smells bad, a person just released from prison, a severely mentally challenged child, an openly gay person. Somebody. I could prowl around in your past and plop that somebody right next to you in church, and you would squirm and maybe leave. We all would. There is a lurking tolerance threshold in even the best of us. Find me a person who says they're perfectly comfortable sitting next to anyone, and I'll show you someone who is lying. We all draw the line somewhere.

People get so mad at Jesus when he returns to Nazareth because he's fiddling around with that line. Jesus is there in his hometown congregation. The members know his mother and his father and have seen him grow up from a young sprout. They ask him to read a lesson in worship that day and he reads beautifully, flawlessly, from the book of Isaiah; he enunciates with the perfect diction of Tom Brokaw. He is the consummate lector. The whole congregation is utterly slack-jawed, full of flattery and amazement at Jesus' performance. The Bible clearly says: "all spoke well of him."

Now why in the world didn't Jesus just soak up the adulation, shake a few hands after worship at the door, and head home for his mom's fried chicken? Why did he have to go and start preaching, meddling with these people? He senses they want him to snap off a few whiz-bang miracles like those down by the sea in Capernaum.

So Jesus launches into a sermon, a pointed commentary on what he's just read from the book of Isaiah. Jesus says something like, "Let me tell you the truth, old friends and neighbors (for that is what they were). Do you remember all those years ago when water was scarce in our land and there was nothing to eat? Do you remember the person old Elijah went to way back when during that horrible drought? Well, I'll refresh your memories. God passed over our people and sent Elijah to an old widow woman who wasn't one of us at all. She wasn't our race, wasn't our religion, and didn't really belong in our story. And yet Elijah was sent to this woman and not to people like us."[16]

And then Jesus preached some more that day. Preaching can be dangerous business. "And surely," he might have said, "you all remember how Elisha, the heir-apparent prophet (you guys know this stuff), could have cured all sorts of our family members of leprosy. But God passed us over again and went and cured another outsider, that foreign fellow who was an officer in the Syrian army. What was his name? Oh yeah, Naaman."[17]

And I don't care if Jesus' aunts and uncles were in the congregation that day. Those people were upset when they heard that sermon, incredibly ticked off. They got so mad that the church service ended right then and there, liturgy over, and congregation members stormed the pulpit. They grabbed Jesus, pushed him out the door, led him to the brow of a cliff, and meant to throw him off. For preaching a sermon! Well, Jesus is somehow able to mysteriously pass through the mob. But there will be another town, another hill, and another mob. And as you well know, he won't be so fortunate next time.

Now why do these folk get so mad at Jesus? They are absolutely furious with the man. Why? Well, you know perfectly well why. As far as I can tell, he was fiddling with that line we were talking about, that line that we all draw. He has dared to suggest that God loves people that we aren't at all comfortable sitting next to, dared to suggest that God even goes out of the way to find these people that we cannot stand.

And if we're honest, that will also make us mad, furious even, because we too cannot imagine such people deserving such attention after what they've done. We cannot imagine it, but am I getting this right? Is this the clincher making people angry enough to kill Jesus? *He told them that God loves people we cannot stand and wouldn't sit next to in church, just as much as he loves us.* He doesn't love them any more than us, of course, but not less. So let's be honest. Are you angry about that yet?

This may be an odd thing to say, but it's possible that unless Jesus is angering you with some regularity, then you might not be reading him all that closely. If he's always the tender, gentle shepherd bouncing children on the knee, a robed, happy, benevolent Santa Claus wandering the hills of Galilee, then perhaps we've really missed what he intends to do in us—change us more and more into his likeness.

In that wonderful passage on love from First Corinthians, St. Paul says that we "have been fully known" (13:12). *Fully known.* It's comforting to be "fully known" by God. It can also be terrifying because if we are "fully known" then nothing can be hidden. Our prejudices, our hatreds, our old, festering wounds and grudges are exposed. Jesus does this about as well as anyone I know. He will lead us to spiritual growth if we listen closely. But trust me on this: *he will first make us angry.* If he doesn't raise our ire on a regular basis, then I suspect that we've settled for a domesticated Jesus who only coddles, affirms, and supports us without condition.

In any congregation in a new century, one finds lots of people who are on the church rolls but participate in community life only occasionally at best. This should cause us great alarm, for I've never met a person who is growing in Jesus apart from the church. People often join the church, make promises, and vanish. If you care about the gospel, you might fret about such folk. You might ask, "Well whatever became of that family? Why isn't so and so attending these days?" You might pray for an individual or a relative whose absenteeism concerns you. People depart and become inactive for a variety of reasons. No one reached out in a time of crisis. The pastor said or maybe did something that was offensive. Feelings were hurt by another church member. Or maybe a general lack of feeling wanted or included caused the departure. When I talk with my pastoral colleagues, those four reasons are usually near the top.

May I add a fifth overlooked reason? And we must come to terms with this particular reason as we seek to welcome new people into any community of faith. Much more often than you might think, people leave a congregation over Jesus. Instead of taking his teachings to heart and allowing the Holy Spirit to form us more and more into Christ's image, it's far easier to flee. Faithful discipleship can be demanding and dangerous because it often means changing how we live and whom we choose to include. Running the other way from Jesus becomes an appealing option. If you've never considered fleeing from Jesus, then it may be that you've never read him with any regularity.

"All spoke well of him." All spoke well of him until he started to preach, until he started fiddling with that line. They loved him as a lector but ran him out of town when he got too close to home.

How shall we receive Jesus into our lives? On his terms or ours?

Sometimes the great good news of Jesus might sound pretty bad to us. His teachings sometimes make us angry enough to spit nails. And then we always have a choice. We would never really push Jesus over the brow of a cliff to get rid of him. Not these days. Americans are too civilized for that.

We would only push him out of our lives so far and so insidiously that, in the end, doing away with the man by ignoring him amounts to about the same thing.

For Reflection and Discussion

· *Someone has said, "Whenever we draw a line between ourselves and another group of people, Jesus is always standing on the other side of that line." Do you agree with this statement? Why or why not?*

- *Describe your own "tolerance threshold." What about the teachings of Jesus make you uncomfortable or angry?*

- *Reflect upon the three examples that open this essay. Does one of the instances cited disturb you more than another?*

Love at First Sight

MATTHEW 4:12-22

HERE IN THE UNITED States, the mind almost always precedes the feet. Now what do I mean by that? I mean that normally we rationally need to examine something, take our time mulling it over, coming to some internal agreement or philosophical justification, before taking specific steps of action. We usually sign on only after we are convinced. This is true about most every decision we make in life, ranging from where we'll go to college to whom we'll marry to whether we'll accept that new job transfer in another town. The mind precedes the feet.

"Convince me," we say to ourselves. In the mental bumper stickers of our minds, that one has to rank up there pretty high. We are naturally skeptical people who need time to think and then take action. I'm not saying this is bad. To be inquisitive and look at life from all angles is actually a fairly wise way to make decisions. Come to think of it, it's the way my best teachers have taught me to look at life. The mind precedes the feet.

It strikes me, then, as very strange, almost bizarre, that the first four disciples, two pairs of brothers, seem to put their feet before their minds. According to the gospel of Matthew, Peter and Andrew are fishing, casting a net into the water. James and John are mending nets—a normal day on the job. Up walks Jesus. It is important to note that these brothers have never laid eyes on Jesus before this moment, nor has Jesus performed any miracles in Matthew that might have attracted attention or padded his reputation. In fact, Jesus is brand new in town. He has just moved to Capernaum from Nazareth. Jesus walks up and says, "Follow me." Without a break in the text, with no internal rumination or even a sleepless night, the four brothers drop everything and take off with this man. Matthew twice uses the word "immediately" to underscore how the response of these fishermen had nothing to do with a rational, well-thought-out decision. Jesus comes along, and they are immediately on the road with him, leaving job and parents and family with no explanation.

I used this story several years ago with several skeptical friends who were helping me with my doctoral project, and one perceptive listener asked, "How do we know Jesus didn't know these brothers? There's a lot that Jesus must have done that's not recorded in the Bible. We have no way of knowing how much contact Jesus did or didn't have with these fishermen before calling them to follow."[18] And that's true, of course. We have no way of knowing. Many people have tried to psychologize the responses of these first four disciples and project feelings and thoughts into their minds that must surely have been part of their decision. For example, what did Peter's wife think? (We're later told he has a mother-in-law so he must have been married, right?) If the brothers didn't own the fishing business outright, what did their employers think about their impetuous decision to simply walk off the job? What about poor Zebedee, their father, who must have been ready for the nursing home, after all?

How did he feel about being abandoned on the beach, left holding the nets? Was he surprised or unhappy with his boys?

All of these questions are endlessly interesting and they underscore the undeniable truth that following Jesus will take priority even over job and family. Jesus asks to be first because he believes that when we make him first he can then help us with job, family, and many other things. Matthew surely wants us to see that following Jesus will mean leaving something behind, and, therefore, it's natural for us to conclude that these brothers needed some time to ponder, ruminate, and scratch their heads before they just dropped it all and struck out on their new lives. Surely they looked at Jesus that day and at the very least said, "Well, yes, following you sounds interesting, sir, but let me think about that overnight and I'll get back to you tomorrow morning." It's a reasonable, sane response, isn't it?

But Matthew doesn't tell the story that way, even though he could have. Even though I wish he had. Matthew says that Peter, Andrew, James, and John dropped everything right there on the spot and "immediately" followed a man who five minutes before had been a stranger. Maybe it was love at first sight, I don't know, but this does not sit well with me. We live a lot of life in our heads and are dubious about most glitzy ideas.

A stranger approaches four fishermen, and they drop everything and immediately follow the man. You expect me to swallow that one? Ha-ha. Tell me another western. It's almost impossible for us who place our minds before our feet to take this story seriously. It could never have happened this way. Such a response would have been foolish, irresponsible, naïve. Who makes decisions this way? We don't make decisions this way, and I don't care if these guys *are* disciples. They should be . . .

And see, when we talk this way about how these first four were called, I believe Matthew's got us just where he wants us. He's exposing precisely how we live so much of our faith in our minds, from the neck up, rationally examining Jesus from a distance, raising good questions and doubts but needing those questions and doubts fully and absolutely resolved before proceeding—needing to know exactly where we're going before striking out into the future with Jesus, we dare to say, in trust.

Surely we come to theological insight about Jesus in just these ways. He did encourage us to love with heart, *mind*, and soul, didn't he? Shouldn't we use our brains before dropping everything to follow this man? Yes, we should. But this story raises unsettling questions for me. What if the way to know Jesus means first following and only later understanding? What if true insight about the man occurs through obediently answering his call and only later looking back to see what it all means?

What would it mean if the man is mainly understood only when the feet precede the mind?

For Reflection and Discussion

- *Consider the major decisions you've made in your life to date. How have you arrived at these decisions? How much risk and trust were involved as you made them?*

- *Which views of Jesus are you willing to trust and follow even as you do so with unanswered questions?*

- *Ask and ponder the question that concludes this essay.*

God's Foolish Choices

1 CORINTHIANS 1:18-31

IN THE UNITED STATES, we love to ask questions about the nature of God. We especially love to ask questions about God when suffering knocks at our door. Such questions are a natural and important part of theological growth and development. So with Perry Mason-like intensity, the interrogation begins. *What kind of God would allow this to happen? Where was God during this illness, that tragedy? What kind of God is this anyway?* God often seems distant to us, even unfair and uncaring, difficult to engage in prayer—aloof, remote. All those questions are endlessly interesting and important questions. We all ask them (pastors included), and the Bible gives allowance and even invitation for such ponderings. God can take it. Fire away.

But in the Book of Micah, in an interesting reversal of how we usually think about these matters, it's not God who's on trial but rather the people of God (6:1-8). And I do mean literally "on trial." God has hauled the *entire congregation* into court. All Israel takes the stand, the whole kit and caboodle of them. The jury? "Hear, you mountains, the controversy of the Lord, and you enduring foundations of the earth." Not a bad choice for the jury—peaks and hills, the earth's hidden foundations. Mountains may not say much, but by golly they listen awfully well.

We may have our own endlessly interesting questions about God, but here in the story of Micah God's got a beef with us. God pleads a case before the mountains. Take the stand. Raise your right hand. Do you swear to tell the truth, the whole truth, and nothing but the truth?

God, the prosecuting attorney, approaches the jury box. Israel is on trial but also us. We're all crammed in there, sworn in as witnesses, awaiting God's first words. And it's hard for me to tell whether sadness or anger most colors these words. God approaches us all. "What have I done to you?" asks God. "Why have you gotten so tired of me?" You can hear the pain in God's words. *What have I done to you? Why don't you come around anymore?* The questions hang there in the silence. "Answer me!" shouts God. And the question echoes all through the jury, across the mountains and hills.

o   o   o

I was on the coast of Georgia recently for a conference on discipleship in a new millennium and one of the leaders, Will Willimon, former chaplain of Duke University, told a story of an African bishop who once visited campus. The bishop described a mass baptism in his country at a huge worship service—two thousand people baptized at one time. When the 1500th person was baptized that day, the African bishop ran out of time and had to leave, which almost caused a riot among the faithful. He promised to return at a later date. At the conclusion of this story, the bishop turned to the university chaplain and said, "And how about you? How many baptisms have you performed here on campus in the last year?" The chaplain scratched his head a moment. "I, uh, I think we had six last year." *Six thousand?* asked the bishop. "Well, no, uh, six." *Six hundred?* the bishop persisted. "Well, no, six total." When this news finally sunk in, the bishop's countenance fell, but then he suddenly perked up. "I know what I will tell my people back in Africa. It's simply amazing. I will tell them that here is a pastor who gets up to speak for God every Sunday *even though God gives him no fruit!*"

"What have I done to you? In what have I wearied you? Why are you tired of me?" It's hard to tell the exact tenor of God's words here in Micah—whether God is primarily sad or angry or maybe just plain hurt. But I do think these words are meant for us, for me— I who am endlessly interested in situational questions about God but far less interested in looking at my own faith habits—questions about me.

The lesson from Micah keeps me on the stand for a while. It's frankly hard to hear. "Do you think I'm happy with your occasional bowing, your seasonal offerings, the sacred oil you pour out in my name?" God bores in on the real problem—going through the religious motions while the heart is far away chasing after false gods: undeniably a huge problem for the American church, undeniably a huge problem for me. "What have I done to you? Why are you tired of me?" Living in America as we do, land of power and might, we can forget who we are. We can forget what church is for. We can forget God until our next big question of him.

So we're all packed in there, all on the stand. Just before we're invited to step down, the Divine Cross-Examiner sums up his case: "I've told you, many times, O mortal, what is good, exactly what the Lord requires of you. But listen and I'll tell you again: do justice, love kindness, and walk humbly with your God." The mountains need not speak a verdict. Their silence and timelessness suggest a certain mercy and patience. But this, apparently, is how we will all be judged in due time—not on the basis of how much wealth and power we've each accumulated, how much prestige we've managed to amass, or how much knowledge we've attained. No, we'll be judged on the basis of our collective passion for justice and care of the poor, our love affair with kindness, and our humble walk with God. This was the very heart and soul of the life and ministry of Jesus.

o o o

Now fast-forward about 750 years. Fast-forward to a certain letter written to a certain church that claimed to follow this very man
who did justice, loved kindness, and walked humbly. First Church in
Corinth was a congregation that had frankly lost its way; it was a sick
church in many ways—religious infighting over things that didn't
matter a whole lot, arguments over who was really in charge, and
bickering over stuff that had very little to do with the love of Jesus.
And so Paul said to himself, "Look, I've had it with these people and
I'm writing a letter—a long letter to address some of this silliness."

And in the very first chapter of that letter, it's as if Paul calls the
whole congregation forward, as Micah once did, crams them into the
witness stand and says, "Now look people, this whole thing called
church isn't really about you or your parents or the traditions you've
started there in Corinth. It's about Jesus—this careless, nonsensical
Jew, a guy most people thought was a clown who died foolishly. And
we have the audacity to stand up and preach about this foolishness,
this cross for wackos, that becomes not weakness in the long run but
actually *power*—power for those who are being saved. And I hope you
noticed that I said 'being saved' because none of you at First Church
Corinth are done yet, and neither am I. We're all works in progress."
My heavens, Paul was on a roll in that letter. I'm telling you, his pen
was on fire.

"I want you to look at yourselves," he continued. "Not many of you
came from high-falutin' families, not many of you are all that powerful, and just a few of you are all that wise to begin with. And even
if you were, none of that crap matters a hill of beans anyway." I would
have loved to have seen the faces of those parishioners the first Sunday Paul's letter was read in church.

"Listen," he wrote. "Listen closely to this nonsense: God chose
what is foolish in the world to show up everybody who thinks they're
wise. God chose a bunch of weaklings to bring the strong to their
knees. And God chose the lowly and despised of this world to show
us all where to really look for his power." These words must have

shocked the pants off people who held multiple degrees from the finest universities in the surrounding Aegean area, multiple land holdings, and multiple allegiances to things other than Jesus.

It's a crazy plan by any reckoning. Imagine a Super Bowl match-up between the Eagles and the Patriots—the fastest, strongest, and most agile football players in the world. We love these titanic clashes of the world's elite. Imagine for a moment that God is a Super Bowl coach, and for a minute, we think that God would dominate any team with 100-yard field goals, perfectly thrown spirals, and a defense that would allow negative total yardage for the entire game. But look again. Here's who God would choose. "God chose what is foolish . . . God chose what is weak . . . God chose what is low and despised." See them out there suiting up? Such a team would be (dare I say it?) *crucified*. (Which may be precisely the point of this old letter from Paul.) "Two bits, four bits, six bits a dollar, all for crucifixion, stand up and holler."

o   o   o

Part of our problem today is that we're looking in all the wrong places for instances of power. We tend to equate power with wealth, might, and prestige. God's idea of power is different. God equates power with weakness, kindness, humility, and the cross. The Beatitudes from Matthew's gospel make absolutely no sense at all to so many residents of our land; they are simply so much foolishness, weakness—fine on paper as little moral maxims, but no way to run a country or even a life.

Our citizenship will often conflict with our discipleship. One fine day in the future, we will be called to the stand to testify before the Truth. That's what our creed says. There will be a reckoning of how we have lived in justice, kindness, and humility. I believe in a God of grace. But the questions from Micah, from God, haunt me. *What have I done to you? Why are you tired of me?*

The questions assume rejection, a certain divine sadness, and the substitution of a false god. The next time you kneel for communion, reflect upon the God who meets us in weakness, whose sacrificial death on a cross trumps all that passes for power in our world. As we receive his body and blood, pray for courage—courage to allow this foolish Jesus to have his way with us all.

For Reflection and Discussion

- *Questions about God are encouraged in any faith journey. But what about God's questions of us? How do you feel about God who judges "the living and the dead"?*

- *The whole idea of the cross of Christ may be very new to you. Even so, what do you make of Paul equating the cross with God's "power"? What sort of power is this?*

- *How do you feel about a God who seems to feel acutely the emotions of rejection and sadness?*

BUT HIS BROTHERS COULD NOT ANSWER HIM, SO DISMAYED WERE THEY AT HIS PRESENCE. THEN JOSEPH SAID TO HIS BROTHERS, "COME CLOSER TO ME." (GENESIS 45:3-4)

8

Come Closer

GENESIS 45:1-15

THE CALL OF GOD TO THE people of Corinth reminds me of another, older story where God brings strength out of weakness—the story of Joseph and his wily brothers. In the verse cited above, Joseph has an important, on-the-spot decision to make. Perhaps you recall details from the story. A coat of many colors. Daddy's favorite son. Sibling rivalry that almost ends in murder. Calmer heads sell the little brother into slavery. The others make up a story for their old man. Joseph is as good as dead.

This is a story as seamy and tawdry as any afternoon soap opera. Read the whole sordid tale sometime soon in Genesis, chapters 37–50. It's no coincidence that the Ten Commandments were handed out in the very next book of the Bible. The main characters in this story flirt with every single "thou shalt not" in the book. My confirmation class recently read the Joseph story from beginning to end. I've never seen them so riveted to Holy Scripture. They wanted to read over and over again the part about Potiphar's wife seducing Joseph, tearing the poor boy's clothes off. This story is like entering a shopping mall of sin and deceit—a virtual catalog, an encyclopedia of despicable behavior: lying, cover-ups, jealousy, guilt, and God. God always seems to be in the thick of scum and dirt in the Bible, have you noticed?

On the verge of starving to death, the brothers head south to Egypt to beg for bread. Standing before them and head of the local Food Bank, in a rich twist of fate, is Joseph—the very brother they had beaten, mocked, sold, and left for dead. Joseph has worked his way up the Egyptian political hierarchy with his intelligence, good looks, faithfulness, and wisdom. And of course these brothers, who would be pulling jail time for their crimes had they been caught and convicted, do not recognize Joseph. But Joseph recognizes them. And it is there, right there, that Joseph has a decision to make.

"I am Joseph. Is my father still alive?" Now, I'd like to freeze the camera on the brothers' surprised faces for just a second. This is the moment of recognition. This is when it hits home to them exactly who this powerful man with a royal scepter really is. I want you to see their faces, their fear, and their urge to run. I want you to see them wetting their pants. Joseph has an advantage that any victim can only dream about. Maybe you have fantasized about such a moment of revenge and retaliation with someone who has hurt you deeply.

Then Joseph said to his brothers, "Come closer to me." I love it. Yes, dear brothers, come closer, just a little closer. And I know why I would want them closer and you do, too. Do you think Joseph enjoyed watching them squirm like worms on a hook? Lewis Smedes has written that when someone wrongs us, "We want the satisfaction of watching him turn and burn with hellish leisure on the rotisserie of his remorse."[19] I wonder if Joseph at least let them hang there long enough to watch the urine puddle at their feet. If you read the whole story you'll learn that he does play around with their emotions a bit.

But it is there, right there, that Joseph has a decision to make. He can seek revenge or he can forgive them. A clear choice. And please don't think revenge wasn't an option. "Come closer, my brothers." Joseph chooses forgiveness even though he had every right to choose retaliation.

Revenge may be among the sweetest of all emotions, but retaliation may send us into an endless cycle that is difficult to control once we've let the "pay-back" genie out of the bottle. We can get mired in plottings and revenge that negatively control us for decades. The current violence between Palestinians and Israelis did not begin yesterday. Both sides are mired in a long history of paybacks. Ditto in Ireland, Rwanda, Iraq, Sudan, and situations all over the world.

I am not trying to minimize the horrible things that humans do to one another in our world—horrible, unspeakable things. I recall a story in a recent edition of our local paper of a Lutheran pastor, a colleague of mine, who was raped twenty years ago and is now bravely speaking out about her past after matched DNA identified the rapist. Humans are capable of emotionally crippling others for life. Unfortunately, there is no "delete key" for the past. So at face value, Jesus' words to disciples do not make sense. "I say to you that listen [Jesus knows these words will be hard to listen to]: Love your enemies, do good to those who hate you, bless those who curse you, pray for those who abuse you" (Luke 6:27-28). Read these four imperatives slowly. Let them sink in. Why would Jesus suggest doing these things? Perhaps because he knows something we forget. He knows that the person who is truly damaged through a festering grudge is the very person who has been wronged: the innocent victim. "Most of our getting even," says Lewis Smedes, "happens only in our private fantasies . . . and our fantasies become a catheter dripping a spiritual poison into our systems."[20] Hatred will literally eat you alive from the inside out.

"Come closer to me," says Joseph. And they came closer. It was there, right there, that Joseph had a decision to make. No one could make the decision for him. No one could force him to conclude that God had somehow been present and active even in those dark times. No one could "guilt" Joseph into forgiving his brothers. Please remember all three of those things when talking with someone who is struggling with forgiveness. Forgiveness may take a long time to happen, if ever. And remember also that there are some things, perhaps, that only God can forgive, even as we release our anger toward that person.

Joseph, with God's help, made a conscious decision to interrupt the cycle of revenge that keeps so many people in their own private jails, "the catheter dripping spiritual poison." How do we find the courage to forgive someone?

o o o

"Closer," whispered a man hanging on a cross. We were all gathered there at his feet, looking up, guilty as charged. "Come closer to me, I have something to say." It was there, right there, that Jesus had a decision to make.

"Father forgive them," he prayed. "They know not what they are doing."

None of us is Jesus. But by watching him and drawing close to his life, perhaps we learn something of how to practice the miracle of forgiveness.

Closer. Come closer.

For Reflection and Discussion

- *Scan the entire Joseph narrative in Genesis, chapters 37-50. Take several notes concerning the general family dynamics.*

- *Reflect upon this old line from the Lord's Prayer: "Forgive us our trespasses, as we forgive those who trespass against us." What is the relationship between divine and human forgiveness?*

- *Even if you never share this with anyone, take a moment to write about another person who has wounded you deeply. What were your honest thoughts and feelings in the early days of that betrayal?*

9

Holy Listening

MATTHEW 17:1-9

LET'S BEGIN IN A RATHER odd place—in the dirt, on the ground. The Transfiguration story occurs on a mountain, a place normally associated with beauty. And three disciples do indeed see something beautiful up there. But for a chunk of this tale they are on the ground; they literally hit the dirt and cover their heads. I suppose this may seem like a rather obvious question on one level, but I want you to think about this with me. *Why do these disciples bite the dust in this story?* You don't have to look very hard to discover that they are afraid. In fact, the story says that they were "overcome by fear." I take that to mean they almost fainted. And so down they go. But what *exactly* are these disciples afraid of? I know what you're thinking. It's not every day that one hears a voice thunder from the sky. Maybe we'd all hit the ground upon hearing such a voice. But is that the real reason our trio is so filled with fear, so overcome? Is it the voice? Be thinking about this. I'll come back to it.

Each May for the last fifteen years, I've taken a weeklong bicycle trip with a group of guys on the Blue Ridge Parkway. We camp, carry tents and sleeping bags lashed to the bicycle, and gain and lose enough elevation in that week to tax heart, lungs, and a posterior now approaching the half-century mark. It's great fun (if you like this sort of thing), and we usually see an abundance of flora and fauna easily missed from a car. I like to think that one of the reasons Jesus took those disciples with him on a hike up a mountain that day was to remind them of the beauty (abundant beauty) that is all around us if we take time to pay attention.

Dorothy Sayers once said that worship is "learning to pay attention." I really like that definition. If we watch closely, altars abound. Altars are everywhere, places where we might kneel in wonder, praise, thanksgiving, and confession.

Well, one time on this bicycle trip I was coasting along the Parkway, enjoying a gentle downhill, and a bear crossed the road about thirty yards in front of my bike, just slowly ambling along. It hadn't even noticed me yet. I haven't seen that many bears in the wild—maybe five. They are usually rather timid and shy in my part of the country. So upon sighting this one, what did I do? I squeezed the brake levers, turned to my companion, and yelled, "Bear! Hey, did you see that bear? Not a very big bear, an older cub, but did you see it? What do you think that bear weighed? 150 pounds? That was incredible! We saw a bear!" And, of course, no one else in three counties saw a bear that day.

When Hannah, our oldest, was born in Winchester, Virginia, a little over twenty years ago, I remember standing at the maternity ward window and staring at her in wonder. A stranger came to peek at the babies, and we stood in silence awhile together. I couldn't stand it and finally said something like, "Yeah, she's the one back there, seven and a half pounds, twenty-one inches long, with an Apgar score of nine." Mystery explained.

Or listen to our words at a funeral home, filing by the body: "Doesn't she look good? I think she looks great. Don't you? They did such a good job. She looks so peaceful, so at rest. Don't you think? That's a beautiful dress. She loved that dress. Blue was her favorite color." Don't get me wrong. These sorts of words are also my words. When looking upon a mystery, it's tough for us to be quiet. We fill up the silence with words.

When the disciples climbed that mountain with Jesus, you know what they saw. They paid attention in confirmation class and knew who those guys were—the very pillars of the Old Testament, here, on this mountain. "My heavens," they must have thought. "Does Jesus know *them*? Does he hang out with *these* two guys?" They stood there with their mouths open awhile, taking in the scene, and Peter finally says, "Whoa! This is amazing! Do you see who's standing over there? Lord, look, this is awesome. You are just too much, man. We've gotta capture this moment—take a group shot, build a picnic shelter, erect a monument. Do you guys see who's standing over there?" Like an elusive bear that crossed the road or a new baby in the window, this scene elicited excited speech from Peter. If worship means paying attention, then Peter was ready to build an altar.

But here comes the line: "While he was still speaking, suddenly a bright cloud overshadowed them, and from the cloud a voice said, 'This is my Son, the Beloved; listen to him!'" And boom, our hiking party hits the deck. See them there on the ground? In the dirt? They are huddled together, afraid. But again the question: afraid of what? There is a scene in *The Wizard of Oz* where Dorothy and company arrive at Emerald City and are finally granted an audience with the great and powerful wizard. The wizard's voice so frightens them that all four flee down the great hall and the Cowardly Lion dives through a window to escape. Is that why these disciples hit the ground? Is it the voice of God that frightens them so? Hold on to that question just a little longer.

In one of his books, Eugene Peterson offers these wise words about God: "Christian spirituality," he says, "does not begin with us talking about our experience; it begins with listening to God call us, heal us, forgive us. This is hard to get into our heads. We talk habitually to ourselves about ourselves. We don't listen. If we do listen to each other it is almost always with the purpose of getting something we can use in our turn. Much of our listening is a form of politeness, courteously waiting our turn to talk about ourselves. But in relation to God especially we must break the habit and let him speak to us."[21]

Even though we worship Jesus, seek an experience with Jesus, make sense of our lives in relation to Jesus, call upon Jesus with a variety of needs, it is undeniably difficult for modern people like us to get quiet and simply listen to Jesus. And this may be especially true for preachers, who are paid to yammer. So recall the voice on the mountain. "Listen to him." *Listen to him.* And the disciples fall to the ground in fear. Why are they afraid? Have you been thinking about this?

I used to think it was indeed that Oz-like voice that sent them into the dirt. But lately I'm convinced it has less to do with the voice and more to do with those three words: *Listen to him.* In your Bible, turn to the sixteenth chapter just preceding this one in the Gospel of Matthew. Just a handful of verses before this story, Jesus clearly describes his destiny to Peter. He's going to be arrested, eventually suffer, and die. And furthermore, says Jesus, anyone who wants to follow me must undergo something similar: deny self, pick up a cross, and get in line.

Do you notice Peter's response? He essentially puts his hands over his ears and says, "I'm not listening. I'm not listening to this. You must be wrong about this, Lord." Six days later, they climb a mountain. On top Peter says, "Hey, this is more like it. Do you see those guys? Do you see them? Let's build something." Peter is beside himself with chattering excitement. And then the voice interrupts Peter, interrupts the words even while Peter is still yammering. "Listen," says the voice. *Listen to Jesus.*

I think if we truly take time to silence the chatter in our lives, turn off the television, and turn off the cell phone; if we truly take time to listen to Jesus and what he is asking of us, we too just might hit the ground in fear—the same ground that will eventually receive us all one day, sooner or later.

o   o   o

It is striking to me that the story does not end on the ground, however. Jesus comes, touches each of the disciples, and says, "Get up and do not be afraid." *Get up.* These are resurrection words, by the way, spoken elsewhere in the New Testament to raise the dead. The verb here, and for risings elsewhere, is one and the same.

I won't lie. If we silence the chatter of our lives and truly listen to Jesus, truly listen to his subversive call, his words are going to bring fear to our lives—fear as well as comfort. That's why those disciples hit the deck on that mountain so long ago. But Jesus still comes to each of us, touches us, feeds us with his body and blood, and says, "Get up." Rise and do not be afraid.

Lent is just around the corner in the Christian year at the point most churches together read this story. The ashen cross we put on our brows to mark the beginning of Lent serves as a reminder of our purpose and destiny as Christ's disciples. We are not protected from suffering and death. It's in the cards for each of us, I'm afraid. And yes, that's it exactly. *I'm indeed afraid.* Listening to Jesus can be a fearful thing sometimes.

An invitation to authentic discipleship is truly enough to make anybody hit the ground. But remember that Jesus has stared death down—his body received into the earth, the ground that we fear the most. His rising from the earth foreshadows our own, and gives us courage.

"Rise," he says. "Get up and do not be afraid."

For Reflection and Discussion

- *Consider taking on the discipline of silence during some part of every day—no TV, conversation, or noise. Simply listen for the voice of Jesus. Why is silence such a difficult discipline for us?*

- *Make an honest inventory of the voices and sounds that saturate a typical day.*

- *Read again the quote from Eugene Peterson quoted in this essay. Think of someone you know who listens extremely well. Consider asking how and why they do this.*

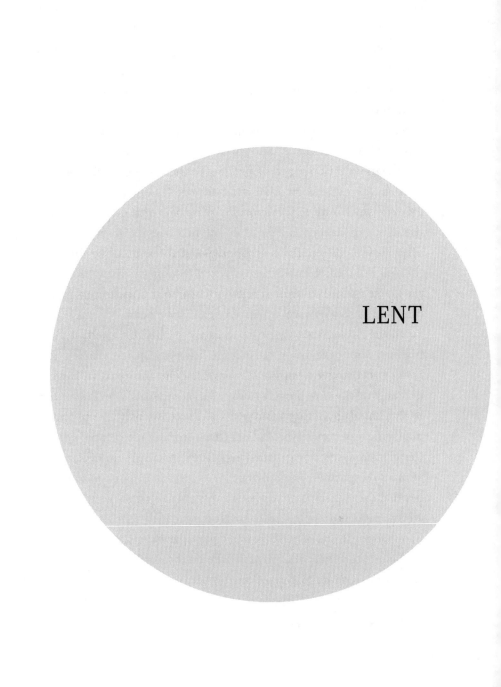

LENT

Lent

On a recent retreat in the North Carolina mountains, another Lutheran pastor said that sometimes when people are behaving badly, we have a tendency to say, "Oh, that's just Henry. That's the way he's always been." In other words, we tend to discount the possibility of change in the person's life and the transformational power of the Holy Spirit to effect that change at any age. We steer clear of certain people and accept their unhealthy idiosyncrasies because that's the way they've "always been" and (presumably) will always be.

Elizabeth O'Connor was a prophet in the wider church before her death several years ago. Listen to her words of encouragement from an early work, *Call to Commitment*: "The deepening of the spiritual life is not spontaneous. People do not just become great Christians. They grow as they make certain purposeful responses to life and to the grace of God. We call these ordered responses 'disciplines.' Like the house thermostat which registers heat, our faithfulness in disciplines indicates how well the fire burns in the heart."[22]

In the Bible, fire (Greek = *pur*, as in "purify") is used as a striking metaphor describing the change Jesus brings to our lives. Jesus is the fire-bringer whose teachings drive out the chaff in our lives, demanding the slow burning away of all competing allegiances. Lent is an annual invitation from Jesus to allow his holy fire to have its purifying way in our lives. In Lent (the word literally means "spring"), the classic disciplines of fasting, study, prayer, service, and worship allow space for the Spirit's cleansing. It's important to remember that these disciplines have no inherent saving value, but they are vitally important, principally for giving the Holy Spirit room to work in our lives. In short, the Spirit is given space to get at us.

No one can twist your arm to take on the disciplines of Lent. We are given freedom to choose our own way if that's our desire. But I trust the old guides. The gospel of Jesus assumes that we *can* change— even the most ornery and cantankerous of God's children.

Piety Practice

MATTHEW 6:1-21

I have a Lenten suspicion. If the Nordic Track people, those gurus of home exercise machines, were to reveal the most popular age for buying some fat-burning contraption, I suspect the age would be about fifty, which I soon will turn. For it is around then that things start to slide south, and one is duped, shamed, goaded into believing that gravity can be overcome with sweat and old-fashioned commitment. We all can be Jack LaLanne if only we work hard enough.

Americans spend a great deal of time maintaining, worrying over, and grooming their bodies—diets, exercise regimens, surgeries. St. Paul does indeed ask in First Corinthians, "Don't you know that your body is a temple of the Holy Spirit within you?" (6:19). It's an excellent question. God calls us to take care of our bodies. But there's so much pressure in our culture to go overboard with upkeep.

My wife, as a sort of joke, has given me the *Sports Illustrated* swimsuit issue each Valentine's Day for the last twenty years. What normal female can possibly look like these women?

While hiking the Appalachian Trail from Maine to Georgia, I once went thirteen days between baths. I wouldn't recommend this for those of you with spouses or day jobs, but for me it was wonderfully liberating. We are bombarded with beauty and fitness pitches that promise outrageous results. You can purchase a device to isolate, exercise, and fine-tune practically any part of your body. Numerous bodily appendages can be shaped and honed by some sort of "Master." I was in Wal-Mart recently and noticed the SlimMaster, the ThighMaster, and the AbMaster. There is actually such a thing as a *Butt*Master. Suzanne Somers swears by the device. It can be yours on Aisle 14 for a mere $49.95.

In the season of Lent it is important to recall that our Lord Jesus Christ is the only true "Master" we'll ever need. On a holy Wednesday we receive an ashen cross on our brows and hear again these profound and ancient words, first uttered by God speaking to Adam way back in the Garden of Eden: "Remember that you are dust, and to dust you shall return" (Genesis 3:19). Adam has, of course, blown it in the obedience department, and this is one of the consequences. "Remember that you are dust." Remember that the worms will go in and out no matter how many crunches you do. Remember that your days are numbered, no matter how much you sweat to extend them. *Remember that you are dust.* It's probably the most honest and accurate thing you'll hear spoken out loud this year. A clergy friend of mine once wrote, "In Lent, we dress our altars, pulpits, and pastors in purple, the annoying color of a bad bruise."[23] In short, Lent forces us to do business with death.

So in light of that dusty truth, the Master gives us some advice. He outlines a regimen. Not a diet/exercise regimen (though that is obviously good for any of us), but rather a spiritual regimen, which is better. You won't find this for sale in any Wal-Mart, but located instead right in the middle of the Sermon on the Mount, Jesus' most concentrated teaching on how to live well in the world. Our Master alludes to three things, three important exercises—almsgiving, prayer, and fasting.

Churches that preach and teach grace, wishing to avoid any hint of legalism, have usually viewed these spiritual exercises—almsgiving, prayer, and fasting—as optional for Lent and life. The truth of the matter is that we have largely lost any real zest for practicing any sort of piety. But notice here that Jesus doesn't say, "If you *choose* to fast, pray, or give alms, be sure to do it this way." He never says, "Once you get around to it, if you happen to opt for these practices, then this is the way it's done." No. Jesus says, "When." "*When* you fast . . . *When* you pray . . . *When* you give away money." These are not optional exercises for a serious Christian. The Master assumes that *disciples* will be about these *disciplines* (note the similarity in the two words). Just as exercise makes our bodies strong, these ancient practices make our spirits strong.

So our Lord assumes that his followers will do without food for periods of time as a reminder that we don't live by bread alone. He assumes that we will give away a definite, sacrificial percentage of our income in order to participate in Christ's redemptive, cross-centered work in the world. And Jesus assumes that we will pray with some regular frequency as a reminder that we can do nothing without the tender mercy of God. Jesus certainly doesn't want us to make a show of these things. He says to "beware" of that. But he does assume we'll do them. The man is simply saying, "You want to follow me? Then here are some practical ways to get at that."

Why is our Lord so adamant about these practices? You don't *have* to do all this stuff to be a Christian, do you?

Author Dallas Willard makes this very important claim: "One of the greatest deceptions in the practice of the Christian religion," he writes, "is the idea that all that really matters is our internal feelings, ideas, beliefs, and intentions."[24] Somehow, somewhere, we have accepted the notion that although it takes hours of sweat and discipline and hard work to maintain a healthy *exterior*, our interior lives magically need no such maintenance. And that is such a very common, yet foolish (and dangerous) notion.

We'll gladly pass out on the ThighMaster or spend hours in search of washboard abs, but we often squawk loud protests when the church suggests fasting or tithing as a means to spiritual maturity. Methinks we protest too loudly. And in so doing we reveal an interest in health that is only skin deep. How can we claim to love Jesus and aspire to follow him, yet ignore his instructions concerning spiritual health?

I once read a story of a father whose daughter, as a teenager, was plagued by terrible bouts of acne. Kids made fun of her. Her face became so ravaged at times that she could not bring herself to leave the house—she was in such anguish. One day her father led her to the bathroom and asked if he could teach her a new way to wash. He leaned over the sink and splashed water over his face, telling her, "On the first splash, say 'In the name of the Father'; on the second, 'in the name of the Son'; and on the third, 'in the name of the Holy Spirit.' Then look up into the mirror and remember that you are a child of God, full of grace and beauty."[25] It was a practice that the girl took into adulthood. No amount of outer therapy can create that kind of inner beauty. Lent gives us wonderful spiritual practices to keep our inner lives in shape.

The disciplines of Lent are not rigid rules. They are gifts to get us in spiritual shape. Without these spiritual practices—fasting, prayer, almsgiving, and others like them—the church will produce puny Christians with few inner resources to truly follow Jesus in the way of the cross.

"Remember," we hear this day. "Remember that you are dust." It is important to take care of your body between now and the dusty future.

But even more important is our attention to developing a spiritual strength that will see us through the days ahead. In a land glutted with Thigh- and AbMasters, it behooves us to listen closely to the real Master.

For Reflection and Discussion

- *How might honest reflection upon our mortality lead one to a healthier perspective on the gift of life?*

- *Reflect upon the close association between the words "discipline" and "disciple." What is a disciple? How do you become one?*

- *How does the church avoid charges of "legalism" on the one hand and "anything goes" on the other?*

2

How Jesus Hangs On

LUKE 4:1-13

IN HIS WONDERFULLY imagined novel titled *Quarantine*, British writer Jim Crace retells the old story of Jesus' forty-day fast in the desert. The setting for a good balance of the novel is a cave where Jesus spends much of each day—cold, alone, and hungry.

No one had said how painful it would be, how first, there would be headaches and bad breath, weakness, fainting; or how the coating on the upper surface of his tongue would thicken day by day; or how his tongue would soon become stuck to the upper part of his mouth, held in place by gluey strings of hunger, so that he would mutter to himself or say his prayers as if his palate had been cleft at birth; or how his gums would bleed and his teeth become as loose as date stones.[26]

Even if you managed to make it through a whole day of fasting last Ash Wednesday, it's still almost impossible to imagine how Jesus did it for forty days. And even harder to imagine how he then resisted the temptations of the evil one. And I might add that these temptations were not obviously *bad* things, but probably to most of us looked like pretty good things—bread, power, and fame. You have to ask how in the world Jesus did it. Did he have some special advantage as God's chosen son? Divine willpower tucked far out of sight to which mere mortals like you and me have no possible access? Given the circumstances, how did Jesus resist the devil? How did he hang on?

Hold on to that question while I take a little detour. When my immediate family gathers at the beach each June—from Iowa, North Carolina, and Tennessee—we usually do two basic things. We eat and tell stories. Everyone knows the stories. Everyone has heard the stories dozens, if not hundreds, of times.

The one about my great-grandfather Frank (I'm named for him) who, as sheriff of Cabarrus County in 1908, presided over the last legal hanging in the state of North Carolina even though he was personally opposed to the death penalty. The story of how my mother and father met on a blind date. The one about how I got lost at the beach for several hours when I was only four. Or how the interstate came through and messed up our woods in the 1960s. How we used to fish for carp with dog food down on Chickamauga Creek, and how I brought back a whopper once in the family orange juice container. The one about my friend Wendell and how he once enticed me to take lawnmower gas and set the front ditch on fire. How my little brother Lee used to eat mud, and how he'd drink half-empty soda bottles from the racks at Cherry Grove Pier if you didn't keep an eye on him.

This is what families do when they get together. They basically eat and tell the same old stories. Everyone laughs and everyone cries.

If you think very long about it, this is what a church family does too. We gather each week to eat around a common table and tell stories that try to make sense of our life together. We tell a little of the story one week and a little more the next. And when we get to the end of the story, we tell it again—maybe with a slightly different twist, but the same story nonetheless. It is this common story that gathers, challenges, and unites us; sends us into the world as different people for having heard and participated in the story.

One very neat thing about this storytelling is that we begin to see ourselves as characters in the plot. Some days I am like Peter, both bold about my faith and other times embarrassed by it. Other days I'm more like Thomas—skeptic and doubter. There's even a part of me that's like Judas. If we tell the story well and if we listen closely to the details, we begin to see ourselves as characters in the plot. The Bible is not inherently magic. But if we pay close attention, the details from our own lives will show up again and again in its pages. It's like an old mirror. Look closely and you'll see your life there. Over time, it is not our political convictions that keep us together. It is not our rather fickle love for each other (or even whether we like each other that much) that ultimately defines our church unity. It really boils down to two things: common food and shared story— word and sacrament.

Now keep this in mind and return to my opening question: *How did Jesus do it?* How did he manage to hang on given the circumstances of a forty-day fast and three very appealing temptations? Let me quickly say this: don't get sidetracked by the existence of a devil in this story. The precise costume that temptation wears isn't important here. In his classic little book about evil, *The Screwtape Letters*, C. S. Lewis writes of a senior devil counseling his nephew in the classic art of deception. Listen in on one letter penned by the uncle: "The fact that *devils* are predominantly comic figures in the modern imagination will help you. If any faint suspicion of your existence begins to arise in his mind, suggest to him a picture of something in red tights, and persuade him that since he cannot believe in that, he therefore cannot believe in you."[27]

So again: don't get sidetracked. It's less important what temptation wears and more important to acknowledge its existence for one and all. Again, here's the central question: *How does Jesus do it?* How does he hang on? Does he rely on his personal willpower, a reservoir of strong mental resistance? Does Jesus act alone and fall back on his own savvy and clever escape mechanisms? Does Jesus raise a magic token of protection that succeeds in warding off the wily tempter? No, on all counts. How does Jesus hang on? He quotes scripture— Deuteronomy to be exact, three times. More specifically, he locates his own tempting situation in the wider story of the Bible: the old wilderness temptations of his ancestors wandering in their own desert. Jesus overcomes temptation by remembering the old stories his congregation used to tell, every Sabbath since he was a very little boy. But I have a hunch. Even though Martin Luther, in his famous hymn, "A Mighty Fortress," claims that "one little word subdues him" (*him* being the devil), maybe you remain skeptical about the power of story. Maybe you find it simplistic to claim that quoting the Bible has the power to send evil packing. And you might even notice that the devil also quotes scripture in this old story.

I often meet parents who say something like, "Religion seems so rigid, and we're so busy, and my child seems well adjusted enough already. Why do we need church?" In a nutshell, here's my answer: so many people I meet simply do not have an adequate story with which to overcome the temptations they will face in the world. And temptations will surely come to us all. Do I need to name them? To be honest, I am usually tempted most powerfully when I mistakenly think that I somehow know what's best for me, my own little life. (Well, guess what? I don't.) To tell you the truth, my own life apart from this old story is pretty boring, fairly pedestrian.

If I do not locate my own life within a much larger story, a much larger picture of the world, I'm liable to live my life according to personal whim, whatever feels good at the moment. We are somehow lured into believing that an insulated, morally neutral life brings happiness. The opposite is most often true. It usually brings misery. It brings misery because our personal, individual story is never large enough to accommodate the complexities of being alive in a world filled with very real temptations. We need an older, bigger backdrop.

In the old television show "The Wonder Years," there was a little boy named Kevin who had a Jewish friend whose name I don't remember. In one episode of the show, this friend celebrates his Bar Mitzvah, which leads Kevin to wonder about his own story. "Mom," he asks, "where do *we* come from?" His mom looks puzzled. "Why don't we ever talk about anything except what's going on with our own family? Why don't we go to church or anything? Why can't I have a Bar Mitzvah?" His questions have never left me.

Many children, sometimes even more than adults, know what is at stake in our world. Moral neutrality is hogwash in this world of powerful temptation and ethical confusion. Our personal, individual stories are never large enough to resist such powers.

Jesus overcomes three very attractive temptations in the wilderness. Coming off an intense, forty-day fast, each must have had its own seductive appeal. How did he do it? How did Jesus hang on? In much the same way we might.

"One little word subdues him."

For Reflection and Discussion

- *Recall several of your family stories that get re-told each year at reunions. How do these stories shape and identify your family?*

- *Share with someone else how you are beginning to see your own history in the pages of the Bible.*

- *What does the word "devil" mean to you?*

"I NOW AM TAKING THIS KINSWOMAN OF MINE, NOT
BECAUSE OF LUST, BUT WITH SINCERITY. GRANT THAT SHE
AND I MAY FIND MERCY AND THAT WE MAY GROW OLD
TOGETHER." (TOBIT 8:7)

In Lust We Trust?

3

TOBIT 8:1-21

THE NEED FOR SPIRITUAL disciplines in the Christian life and their use in overcoming specific temptations faced by all followers of Jesus come together nicely in this next story. After years of preaching and teaching about sin rather generically, I've recently done some prowling around in the ancient breviary of specific slip ups commonly known as "The Seven Deadly Sins," which Gregory the Great, in the sixth century, called "a classification of the normal perils of the soul in the ordinary conditions of life." There is something profoundly liberating about naming certain sins out loud. Particularly has this been true in my own attempt to understand and curb the deadly sin of lust in the "ordinary conditions" of my own pastoral life.

It's hard to find evidence in the Bible that there is somehow part of one's imagination (a hidden slice of it, a fantasy self) that can be kept private and locked away from God. Indeed, each Sunday many Christians confess sin before a God "from whom no secrets are hid." Without question, that short phrase is the most terrifying part of the whole Lutheran liturgy for me. *No secrets.* Couldn't we keep a few? Does God have to know everything about me? Frankly, there is a lot about my life that I would like to keep secret, particularly from God—lots of darkness, judgmental thoughts, and unhealthy cravings, including lust. But the confession is right there in black and white every Sunday: *no secrets.*

This doesn't mean, of course, that Christians should always divulge our darkest and deepest secrets to one another in the name of authentic community. Sometimes that might happen at church in a safe context, but on a regular basis I think such corporate unloading would spell community chaos. There's far too much darkness. As some wise soul has put it, "Judge human beings in a court of law by our thoughts alone and we'd all be thrown in jail." We are complicated, complex people. There are thoughts from our inner lives from which we blessedly shield even a loving spouse.

However, to confess that there are *no secrets* from God means that God includes our inner lives as part of the true geography of redemption. Sin is not just something that we get caught at. Sin is something that is hatched in the heart. A person doesn't say, "My, my, this seems to be a fine Thursday in September on which to go out and commit adultery." Adultery, like most sins ranging from premeditated murder to plagiarism, is hatched in the human heart, rarely a spontaneous thing. That is why Jesus seems so hard-nosed in a passage (Matthew 5:27-28) that tripped up even the likes of Jimmy Carter: "You have heard that it was said, 'You shall not commit adultery.' But I say to you that everyone who looks at a woman with lust has already committed adultery with her in his heart." I've no doubt that Jesus in much the same way is also referring to women lustfully looking at men. It all begins in the heart, where we think secrets can be kept. And yet here's this God from whom *no secrets are hid.* Do we give thanks for such a God or run fast the other way?

I'm certainly not casting stones at anyone who chooses to run. I'm not sure it's possible to be completely free from lust. The Victoria's Secret catalogs arrive in our home, somehow addressed to me, and I must admit that I glance at them (okay, I sometimes stare at them) with something more than pastoral intentions. I still remember the secret stash of *Playboy* magazines that Jimmy, my childhood friend in Chattanooga, collected and stored in a secret, hidden hole in waterproof bags. I can't remember how many times we crept off to the woods to dig them up. Sexual lust is a primordial inclination as old as Eden.

And even though we are hesitant to talk about lust in polite church circles (except to snigger at the sexual sins of someone like Jimmy Swaggart), the Bible is full of sex, lust, adultery, and various exotic proclivities that usually do not make it into the Sunday lectionary. The Bible seems to range between two poles on these matters: sex as a thing of desirous beauty and sex that leads to destruction and heartache.

I'll offer just two biblical examples to illustrate this wide swing. In the Song of Songs, two lovers, two newlyweds utterly devoted to one another, rapturously pour out their hearts with words that are often overtly sexual, littered with lust, and even downright erotic. Garrison Keillor once said that as a young boy he used to read this titillating book of the Bible in bed at night under the covers with a flashlight. Here's just a taste of provocative Holy Scripture from chapter 4: "How beautiful you are, my love, how very beautiful! Your lips are like a crimson thread, and your mouth is lovely. Your two breasts are like two fawns, twins of a gazelle, that feed among the lilies. You are altogether beautiful, my love; there is no flaw in you. You have ravished my heart with a glance of your eyes. Your lips distil nectar, my bride, honey and milk are under your tongue." I could go on (and the text goes appreciably further on!). No matter how hard I try, it's difficult to interpret this passage as symbolically reflecting the love of Christ for his church, as some interpreters have valiantly attempted.

To be honest I have worried quite a bit, even lost some sleep, fretting about biblical illiteracy among our youth. This may be the very thing to get them to pick up the Bible. Assign the Song of Songs. Here the Bible celebrates the beauty of sexual love where partners are carried away with one another in holy rapture and seduction. It rates at least a PG-13.

The other example is from the book of Tobit, an entertaining book considered apocryphal by Protestants, to our great loss. In the tale there is an old couple, Edna and Raguel, who have a beautiful daughter named Sarah. Sarah has been married seven times. Seven different men. Curiously, each man has died on the wedding night at the very moment the marriage was consummated. Word gets out about this, of course, and Sarah's chances for a happy life look mighty slim.

Along comes Tobias, a distant relative, son of the book's namesake, Tobit. Tobias asks for Sarah's hand in marriage. A wedding feast is enjoyed by all. Before they engage in sexual intercourse that night, the happy couple beseeches God for safety. They pray, literally, for safe sex. Here's just part of that remarkable prayer: "Blessed are you, O God of our ancestors, and blessed is your name in all generations forever . . . I am now taking this kinswoman of mine," prays Tobias, "*not because of lust*, but with sincerity. Grant that she and I may find mercy and that we may grow old together" (8:4-7).

They both say "Amen, amen" and go to sleep for the night. Blissfully, the newlyweds see the sun come up and survive their first roll in the hay. So certain, however, that he will have an eighth dead son-in-law on his hands, old Raguel rises in the middle of the night to dig a grave. He is embarrassed by the past funerals so Raguel calls his wife Edna and says with obvious resignation, "Send one of the maids and have her go in to see if he is alive" (8:12). Raguel wants to dispose of the body under the cover of darkness. But this newest son-in-law survives his wedding night, and they live happily ever after. I'm not making this up. It's a Bible story. But the jury is out as to exactly what it means. I don't really know what to make of this tale other than to say the writers must have believed that sexual intercourse could be dangerous and maybe even cost you your life.

Saint Paul was apparently intimately aware of a certain tradition in the book of Numbers when he wrote these words to the church in Corinth: "We must not engage in sexual immorality as some of them did, and twenty-three thousand fell in a single day" (1 Corinthians 10:8). That's three times the population of a Virginia town I once lived in, by the way. God intends that human sexuality should be channeled within certain prescribed parameters.

It's admittedly hard for a young person not to contest these rules, however, when someone like Solomon in the Old Testament is reported to have had numerous wives and concubines with whom he must have enjoyed various and sundry pleasures. Here's a line from First Kings that takes one's breath away: "Among his wives were seven hundred princesses and three hundred concubines; and his wives turned away his heart" (11:3). I can't imagine how. A case could be made that the man was more profligate than Hugh Hefner.

Mark Twain also observed the cruel contradictions of the Bible in his irreverent and funny book, *Letters from the Earth*, published posthumously in 1962. The book is a fictional series of letters penned by Satan who is reporting on the "human-race experiment." This is an excerpt from Letter VIII: "'Thou shalt not commit adultery' is a command which makes no distinction between the following persons. They are all required to obey it: Children at birth. Children in the cradle. School children. Youths and maidens. Fresh adults. Older ones. Men and women of 40. Of 50. Of 60. Of 70. Of 80. Of 90. Of 100. The command does not distribute its burden equally, and cannot. It is not hard upon the three sets of children. It is hard—harder—still harder upon the next three sets—cruelly hard. It is blessedly softened to the next three sets. It has now done all the damage it can . . . Yet with comic imbecility it is continued, and the four remaining estates are put under its crushing ban. Poor old wrecks, they couldn't disobey if they tried."[28]

Despite these objections found within the Bible itself, in the Song of Songs and book of Tobit we discover two, basic, repeated, biblical polarities—the joy of sex versus the threat and real danger of sex. It is obviously difficult for humans to tell the difference. Why?

Lust clouds our judgment. The Bible is full of such clouded judgment ranging from the stories of David and Bathsheba (and Amnon and Tamar) in Second Samuel to the woman at the well in John's gospel. As Eugene Peterson has noted, "The subtlety of sin is that it doesn't feel like sin when we're doing it; it feels godlike, it feels religious, it feels fulfilling and satisfying."[29]

It even feels like an urge where we just can't help ourselves. If you've seen the movie *Oh, Brother, Where Art Thou?*, directed by the Coen brothers, you'll recall the scene where the sirens lure the boys to the water. Lust sends them jumping out of the car and tearing through the woods like hounds in heat. Supposedly, it's a scene straight out of Homer's *Odyssey*. They are powerless to resist the siren call.

But what resources does the Christian faith offer to those struggling with inappropriate lust? Are we powerless? How do we indeed resist? First, I want to return to the idea of a God from whom "no secrets are hid." Jesus cannot be Lord over 75 percent or 93 percent of our lives. The word "Lord" implies that Jesus reigns over our *entire* lives—our furtive thoughts, our clandestine website glimpses, and our secret longings. Following a Lord who knows so much about us does not mean that Jesus is waiting to pounce when we make mistakes or take a second admiring look at a man or woman. It does mean that he cares deeply about the whole self because it is the whole self that gives praise to God. Jesus wants to know about the entire me, even the darkest sides of me, not just the "me" I choose to reveal.

Second, I think we should be reminded again and again that the church is a community of forgiveness and grace. We can start over. Sexual sins can be devastating to a marriage or to the health of a family, but Jesus, please note, does not rank sexual infidelity or unhealthy lust at the top of a list of sins (even though the church often does). The church should never forget the story (even if textually suspicious) of the woman caught in adultery who was discovered in the very act and brought before Jesus (John 8:2-11). We tend to point more fingers at sexual sins than other mistakes.

In the novel *The Good Priest's Son*, the wise aging Episcopal priest, Tasker Kincaid, upon hearing a confession concerning lust from his son, Mabry, observes that sloth is always at the root of the other deadly transgressions: ". . . my observation after sixty years of close sin-watching is that pure *laziness* tops the list. Most people persist in all the other wrongs just because they're too satisfied with lying motionless on their bed or couch—or the couch in their *mind*—to stand up and change."[30]

There is power in knowing that change is possible, that shame and guilt can be confessed before a God who knows our secrets; we can be restored and forgiven. Our acts may have consequences that we cannot take back. That is undeniably true. But the church should not throw stones at wounded people. We all have a shady past of one sort or another—each of us.

And maybe knowing those two things—a God who knows our hidden secrets *and* who is willing to restore us even in light of that—is enough to help us overcome sexual temptation whatever form it might take.

Perhaps St. Paul sums up this particular deadly sin better than anyone. "I do not understand my own actions," he says. "For I do not do what I want, but I do the very thing I hate. . . . Now if I do what I do not want, it is no longer I that do it, but sin that dwells within me. . . . Wretched man that I am! Who will rescue me from this body of death? Thanks be to God through Jesus Christ our Lord!" (Romans 7:15, 20, 24-25).

This is at least part of Paul's powerful promise: Christ's cruciform passion for us will ultimately reveal and overcome our secret, unhealthy passions for others.

For Reflection and Discussion

- *Try to write a short definition of the word "sin." Take a moment and look up "The Seven Deadly Sins" in a computer web search.*

- *Read through the "Song of Songs" (also called the "Song of Solomon") for an example of rapturous romantic love in the Bible.*

- *How is Jesus beginning to re-shape and find access within your inner life and imagination?*

"... BUT OF THE TREE OF THE KNOWLEDGE OF GOOD AND EVIL YOU SHALL NOT EAT, FOR IN THE DAY THAT YOU EAT OF IT YOU SHALL DIE." (GENESIS 2:17)

Two Trees

GENESIS 2:15-3:24

I'VE LOST TRACK OVER the years of the number of people who've said something like the following to me: "You mean you really *believe* in that old story of Adam and Eve? Who could possibly swallow such a tale? Please," they say with a breezy confidence, "I gave up that story years ago along with Jack and Jill and a cow jumping over the moon."

And I suppose on one level the modern detractors of the opening chapters of Genesis are correct. If you try to use the stories to explain the scientific origins of the world from a biological, chemical, and evolutionary perspective, the stories may not be all that satisfying. In a laboratory, Genesis doesn't quite gel with what we know about quantum physics and carbon dating.

But yes, I do believe in "that old story" of Adam and Eve. It may not tell me precisely how the world came to be, but there are few stories that tell me more about how human beings are prone to be. The lab is fascinating. I love science. But I'll take Genesis any day to help me understand, well, *me*. It's my story, our story, and it's as modern as this afternoon, revealing a theme that is perhaps the granddaddy of all temptations: to be your own god.

And so they were told not to eat a certain fruit. All other fruits were okay but this one tree was off limits. Don't eat it. Don't touch it. Don't even think about it. *Verboten*. Any second-grader can figure out the plot here. It's like waving a red flag under the nose of a bull. That which is forbidden becomes overwhelmingly appealing. Any parent knows the psychology at work here. "Now Sally, Joe, you can do anything you want to, with the exception of this." And of course "this" is just too much to resist. We are infatuated with the forbidden like moths drawn to a flame, spending much of our lives dancing around the rarefied air of the prohibited. From a sales perspective the best thing that can happen to an author is to have his or her book banned.

Growing up in Chattanooga, there were some wonderful woods near my house that were even more wonderful before the interstate, I-75, came along. We were let loose to roam and explore the woods, hundreds of acres of small creeks and hills. There was only one rule. "We don't want you going anywhere near Mrs. Connor's house," my parents said. "You can go anywhere but there." Mrs. Connor was the widow of a man who had developed our entire neighborhood from their family farm. She still lived alone in a small cottage, off by itself, surrounded by these woods. No one ever said out loud why to avoid Mrs. Connor's house, but it was widely known among us children that she was a witch. She lived alone in the middle of the woods and must have been up to something strange, we figured. It was a fairly clear rule: "Go anywhere but there." And of course you know exactly where we went. It became a game to see how close we could approach the house on each subsequent visit before running away in total fear. I think my friend Jimmy once touched her porch. That took some guts to touch the porch of a witch. We were certain he would be forever frozen into a statue on the spot.

"All the fruit you see in this garden is yours for the tasting, but you see that one tree over there? See it? Don't eat that fruit. Don't even touch it. Don't even think about it." And the rest is history. Well, forgive me, but in this story God seems fairly out to lunch. I don't mean to be disrespectful or anything, but what was God thinking? God may as well have delivered a *basket* of the forbidden fruit to Adam and Eve's front porch as a housewarming present. It doesn't take a rocket scientist to figure how this is going to work out. One may even wish to ask the obvious: If God didn't want these two to eat that fruit, *then why did he make that tree in the first place?* One writer wonders: "If this was all a test of the first couple's obedience, then why didn't God let them work up to it a little? Start out with something less significant such as: 'Don't call me after 9 P.M.'"[31] That's how a good story works, by the way. It gets under our skin from several different vantage points. Here's one vantage point. Come with me down this particular trail.

All good parents have rules when it comes to raising their children. Children need limits and boundaries. But all parents also know that as children get older and wiser, they begin to question the rules. And there comes this strange time when enforcing the rules with increasing severity can sometimes push a child to dance across the threshold just to see what will happen. "Sin is a hereditary disease," said Saint Augustine, "and we are forever in want of a cure." And so parents come to that nerve-wracking but necessary period in their child's life. From the parents' perspective it's called "trust." From the child's perspective it's called "freedom." And no one has ever worked out a completely balanced strategy of rules, trust, and freedom. Tilt the balance out of whack just a bit, and the parent becomes a tyrant. Tilt it the other way too far, and the child quickly learns that complete freedom can lead to agony and lots of hard lessons.

This old story in Genesis works in a very similar fashion. God is striking a good *parental balance* here even though we know things will not turn out well for our garden kin. They had it all—frolicking in a garden full of kumquats, kangaroos, and koala bears. But they will soon find themselves outside the garden, tossed out on the curb of a new life, wondering where it all went wrong. God provides rules and God provides freedom. For humans to thrive we need both. The agonizing thing is that nobody can tell us that, and no one can protect us from these consequences. We will need to learn much of this in the school of experience and hard knocks.

We really are free—free to make bad decisions. And no matter how much we try to blame things on others, or even on God, the large majority of human misery can be laid at our feet. We all worship at the altar of Bad Choices, things that look pretty darn good at the time but in reality very often have lifelong disastrous consequences. I don't think I need to name these temptations out loud. Our own familiarity with the territory is well documented. God could remove our ability to make the poor choice, of course, but we would then be talking about robot-hood rather than a human being; same for Jesus out there in the wilderness early in his ministry. He was not preprogrammed to make the right choice. These were real and enticing temptations. Take away human will and choice, and we're talking about something other than life as we know it. C. S. Lewis once noted, "God cannot ravish. He can only woo."[32] I take that to mean that God refuses to make us do the right thing. Our love for God must be a choice, or we're talking about something other than real love.

A lot is going on in this old story. But one of the main lessons here is that God creates a world where we are free to choose a life without God. We are free to "go it" on our own. We are free to experience the consequences of living life the way *we* think it ought to be lived. We are even free to be our own god.

∘ ∘ ∘

The story of Adam and Eve, of course, is horribly stunted when we try to date it, verify its history, or find archeological evidence for the Garden of Eden. This is *our* story. And I believe the story is "true" because I see my own rebellious self there. *We are Adam and Eve*—blessed with freedom, prone to rebellion, drawn to the forbidden. When the devil tempts Jesus in the wilderness, please remember how exactly he sends the devil packing. Jesus quotes the Bible, using words that are not his own. Even Jesus did not survive out there on his own—he needed a tradition and a scriptural voice.

God has given us an amazing garden in which to live. So many people think that following their own voice, taking their own path, will lead to eternal happiness. The church says otherwise. The church says taking the path of Christ will bring meaning and purpose—learning how to live from others, not just an internal best guess.

Lent is a reminder that we are always free to reject the ways of Jesus. No one can twist our arms. Nor can we be protected from the consequences of insisting upon having our own way.

One of the great paradoxical mysteries of our faith is this: even though an ancient primordial tree stands at the center of our common downfall, another tree stands at the center of our liberation and forgiveness—the "tree" that is the cross. You might think about these two trees this Lent.

We are forever in the thrall of the first tree's shadow, and forever in gratitude for the second tree's light.

For Reflection and Discussion

- *Share a time from your past when you flirted with the forbidden. Why does the forbidden draw us so?*

- *Reflect upon these thoughts from the essay: "No one has ever worked out a completely balanced strategy of rules, trust, and freedom. Tilt the balance out of whack just a bit and the parent becomes a tyrant. Tilt the other way too far . . ."*

- *Talk with a friend about human freedom and C. S. Lewis's quote: "God cannot ravish. He can only woo."*

5.

Jesus and the Evening News

LUKE 13:1-9

THE FOLLOWING sce-
nario did not happen in
the way I'm about to tell it.
But it could happen to any
pastor of my acquaintance.

It is night. The telephone
rips the darkness. The voice on
the other end is an emergency room
nurse who shares the barest outline of a bad
wreck out on the interstate. The family is from out-of-state. They are
Lutherans, says the nurse. Their daughter is in critical condition;
the prognosis is poor. Could I please come right away?

I see them huddled in the corner of the waiting room. Tears. Sob-
bing. Great fear and anxiety. We pray together and then talk. The
story pours out in waves. One of them says, "Pastor, why did this
happen? Why would God allow this to occur? Did we do something
to deserve this?" The questions are as old as human speech. But for
me the questions always seem new and unnerving. I do the pastoral

thing. I assure them that I don't believe in a God like that. We talk some more. I learned in seminary how to handle these situations.

But what if I had taken a course in pastoral care from Jesus himself? What if I had said, "No, heavens no, you didn't do anything to deserve this. God doesn't work that way. But let me be honest with you—unless you people repent pronto, then you too will be maimed and die just like this." Does that sound harsh? Does that sound unfeeling? Well Jesus our Lord said as much once upon a time. Mr. Compassion himself. Maybe he would have failed pastoral care in seminary, but he said it.

Some people approach Jesus in this unsettling story. They've heard some rather disturbing news about a group of innocents who died unjustly under Pilate's reign of terror. Fast-forward several centuries, and they might have said, "Hey Jesus, those 192 people who died in the bombings over in Madrid. Were they worse sinners than all the other Spaniards because they died in such a horrible way?" Jesus scratches his beard a moment. "No, I tell you, there's no connection between the bombing and their behavior. But listen up, people: unless you repent, you too will die in a similar way." You could've heard a pin drop. He has their attention. He lets the silence sink in awhile.

And then Jesus looks out over the rest of the crowd. He remembers an incident about a collapsed tower over at the pool of Siloam. Fast-forward several centuries and his words might have sounded something like this: "And I know what you're probably thinking," he might have said. "What about all those people in Pakistan who recently died from the horrible earthquake there? Were they somehow worse offenders than other Pakistanis? Absolutely not. Now get that crazy idea out of your head. But I will say this: unless you repent, a collapsed tower is also in your own future."

Am I accurately reporting the gist of this story? If you ask me, it's one of the most befuddling tales about Jesus in all of the gospels, much like riding a roller coaster. I find myself cheering and then cringing, at almost the same time. Cheering as Jesus confronts the common notion that sin and suffering are always related. *Yaaay*,

Jesus! You tell 'em a thing or two! Cringing as he predicts a similar future demise unless these people clean up their acts. *Yikes! This isn't the Jesus—kind, loving, and good—I've come to know.*

It's worth pointing out that the two situations of suffering addressed by Jesus could have come right off the evening news. The first situation concerns suffering hatched by a powerful political despot, in this case Pilate. But you could just as easily insert another modern name—Hitler, Stalin, Pol Pot, bin Laden, Hussein. In the first story, Jesus is addressing suffering born of planned malice. Suffering hatched in the heart—willful, calculated evil. Flip on NBC each evening and nary a night will pass without some detailed description of intentional malice visited upon innocents.

But Jesus also addresses a second story. This type of tragedy is not planned by anyone. It just happens and people get in the way—tornadoes, earthquakes, hurricanes, drought. These, too, arrive with regularity on the evening news, and reporters like Tom Brokaw give us as much detail as we're able to stomach. This type of suffering is different from the first in that nobody is responsible, even though insurance companies still refer to such incidents by the curious phrase, "acts of God." Maybe the tower of Siloam fell on those eighteen because the local contractor cut too many corners. But we aren't told that. In this second type of suffering, there is usually no one to blame.

So the two news stories cited by Jesus pretty much cover the waterfront of all suffering—either suffering inflicted by intentional malice or suffering experienced by random chance. In Jesus' day (and still in ours to some extent) there was a strong case made between suffering and sin. If something bad happened to you, there must be a good cause-and-effect reason for that. We applaud Jesus for confronting these misguided people who seem to suggest that God is lowering the boom, sending suffering to the wayward. *Yaaay, Jesus! Tell it like it is!* And so we are drawn in, maybe sucker-punched into the argument, and don't even see the knockout coming. What could Jesus possibly mean by these strange words? "Unless you repent, you will all perish just as they did."

I read a wonderful little essay on fasting recently that gets at the truth of today's gospel lesson. The author of this essay was on Day Six of a weeklong fast. Let me offer a bit of his journal entry for that day: "A guy across from me on the train tears through a Big Mac and two bags of French fries as if his life depended on it. I watch him shovel greasy fries into his mouth, where a fragment of special sauce glistens on his lip. I am revolted. A feeling of, admittedly, pharisaical superiority comes over me. Compared to this guy, I am pure spiritual fire."[33] If you've ever done any fasting, you'll recognize the humor here.

Here's one of the truths of the Christian life that consistently confronts us all: it's far easier to observe evil in others than it is to confess evil in ourselves. Just open a newspaper. Just click on the evening news. Any number of heinous stories abound to remind a viewer to conclude the following: *I may make mistakes, I may hurt people occasionally, I may cut an ethical corner or two. But hey, at least I'm not as bad as this miserable guy.* The people who make the headlines undeniably help us justify our own indiscretions. It's not that difficult to spot and name the bad guy on the evening news. It's often a lot harder to spot the insidious evil in ourselves (or, conversely, easier to hide it).

There was a really funny guy in one of my former youth groups named David. He told me that his older brother Jonathan once racked up $1500.00 in charges on the monthly family phone bill back in the early days of the Internet, when web time was charged like any other long-distance phone call. The phone bill arrived and like any good father, theirs hit the roof. Jonathan, the culprit, was in major hot water. David told me that he got incredible mileage out of this incident for months. For whenever his parents lowered the boom for some infraction of his own, he could always play his ace in the hole: "Well, I'm sorry! But at least I didn't do something as boneheaded as my brother!" David confessed to me that this ploy worked reasonably well for quite some time.

It's easy to justify our own indiscretions as we compare them to other headline-grabbing news. It's tempting to hide our sinful lives amongst the rogues and international tragedies that bombard our senses through radio, television, and print media. Our little sins pale in comparison, don't they?

Jesus will not let us off the hook so easily. Even though we are endlessly interested in asking questions about suffering—whether contrived or accidental—and endlessly fascinated about the "hows" and "whys" of human evil and the God who seems to allow it (quickly pointing out evil here, there, and yonder—even naming the "axis of evil" in the world today), Jesus won't play that game. He turns our questions about evil "out there" and "over there" on their heads, and wants to know about the evil inside each of us, all of us. Jesus refuses to linger with the headlines. He takes aim elsewhere: *at our own lives.* How we each stand before God.

That's why Jesus follows this story with a parable about a fig tree. He's more concerned about the fruit in our own lives, rather than the lack of it in others. Who's to say, after all, that the collective sin of so-called "good" people does not do more damage to the ecosystem, more damage to the hope of eradicating global poverty, and more damage to race relations than a boatload of evil villains and a century's worth of natural disasters? Jesus wants disciples to recognize that it's not just the headlines that define the world's problems. It's us. We're all part of the problem: "For three years," says the vineyard owner, "I have come looking for fruit on this fig tree, and still I find none."

It is tempting to watch the evening news and shake our heads sadly. I won't deny that we live in a messy, bloody world. But Jesus doesn't seem overly concerned with these questions. And if you think about it, shaking our heads doesn't really change anything anyway. Jesus knew this. His real power can never be revealed in wiggling his divine nose and zapping the world into peace and harmony. His real power is revealed in repentance and forgiveness, one person at a time. "Unless you repent, you will all perish just as they did." It's not a threat, but it is the truth.

Shaking our heads at the headlines won't change a thing. Looking deeply into our own fickle hearts and allowing Jesus full access there, will.

For Reflection and Discussion

- *How does the evening news serve to distract us from the sin and evil within ourselves?*

- *Why is it often easier to observe evil in others rather than confess it in ourselves?*

- *Lutherans generally prefer "corporate" confession on Sunday mornings, but pastors do offer "Individual Confession and Forgiveness," which includes absolution and the laying on of hands. If you think it might be helpful, ask your pastor about this rite.*

"come and see a man who told me everything i've ever done." (john 4:29)

All We've Ever Done

JOHN 4:1-42

SOMETIMES I JUST don't understand Jesus. Usually, he seems like a loving, caring Savior, looking out for our best interests and all. He goes out of his way for people and stands up for the little guy. He sides with the unpopular and crosses the tracks when others won't. He's a friend of outcasts. You go, Jesus! He's our man.

But then there's this other Jesus. At times he does things that absolutely shock our modern sensibilities. He says things out loud that we would never *ever* say. He drags things out in the open that we only whisper about. At times Jesus seems like Howard Stern with a Bible. He'll say just about anything. We cringe and wish there was a ten-second delay button we could use to edit these rather rude pronouncements.

For instance, take the old story of the woman at the well. It's the longest recorded conversation between our Lord and another person in any of the gospels. Longer than any single chat he had with his disciples; longer than anything he said to any of the officials who finally killed him; longer even than any recorded conversation he had with his mother. This meeting at a well is a long, nuanced give-and-take, a feast of details and teaching possibilities, enough to keep a student of the Bible busy for years. But for now I want to focus mainly on just one thing: this surprising and rather shocking side of the man we call Lord.

The story begins in a way we've come to expect—Jesus reaches out to a woman who was doubly discarded. First, she was a Samaritan. You may know that Jews and Samaritans were not all that fond of one another. There was a hatred that stretched back to the days of the exile when Samaritans intermarried with foreigners, and Jews like those in Jesus' family remained pure. Samaritans were seen as half-breeds and sellouts. It was a pretty radical act for Jesus to cross over to a whole town of them. Jesus once told a story of a Good Samaritan who became the epitome of what it meant to be a neighbor. People were shocked and scandalized when they heard such a tale. This woman has one strike against her already.

And strike two is close behind. Didn't Jesus know that you didn't talk to a woman in public back then, right out in the open at the town well? Notice verse 27 of this story. Upon returning from buying groceries and snacks in the city, the disciples are "astonished," absolutely shocked to see Jesus talking with a woman out in the open.

There are few stories in the Bible that suggest a more radical and loving inclusion than this one. Jesus was at a well. We've got a baptismal font. Get it? This is one of the reasons I've fallen in love with Jesus. He simply thumbs his nose at divisions of any kind and shows us how to live from God's point of view. I've got a long way to go in living that way, but I do see the truth in it.

What I do not see coming is the next scene in this story. Jesus and this outsider have a nice chat at the well. The woman is a little confused at first, but give her some credit. Jesus offers something called "living water," a spring gushing up into eternal life. And she wants some of that and even asks for it. She knows she's thirsty and knows Jesus has something special. So give her credit. When I'm feeling really grim, I wonder about how many of us church people ever make it that far—to name our thirst honestly and realize who can really quench it. This woman has come a distance with Jesus in just a short conversation. She has made strides.

So watch closely here. What does Jesus do with her heartfelt request? Does he embrace her on the spot and make her a disciple? Does he commend her for such insight? Does he make her a voting member of a local congregation and put her on a church commit-tee? No, on all counts. Jesus becomes Howard Stern with a Bible: The Shock Messiah. He shifts gears so abruptly that you can almost hear them grind. He says, "Uh yeah, by the way. Where's your husband? Bring him over. I'd really like to meet him." Jesus knew the answer to this question already, and probably knew her embarrassment. Does he just want to watch the woman squirm? "I have no husband," she admits. And here Jesus really bores in. "Bingo. You've actually had five husbands, lady," says Mr. Compassion, "not counting the guy you're shackin' up with these days."

Can you imagine Jesus saying such a thing? What in the world is he thinking about? That stuff is none of his business, is it? It's her personal life, all in the past. Why bring it up now? They've just met only fifteen minutes ago! He might offend her and scare her away from the faith. Can you imagine any pastor trying this conversation tactic on a prospective member visit? I'd say New Member Sundays would be few and far between (or maybe a lot more interesting).

At first, the woman shies away from this direct talk. She does what we all do when someone bores in on the truth. She changes the subject. She tries to start an argument about the true place of wor-ship. "We say it's supposed to happen on a mountain. You guys say Jerusalem." She opens an old sectarian wound between Jews and Samaritans and tries to start an argument, diverting attention away from herself. I do this all the time. When my wife gets really close to exposing me for the horse's tail I sometimes am, when she gets really close to some truth about me that I could profitably hear and learn from, I may just start a little argument to divert her. We may not be aware of this, but it's a fairly common strategy. My wife gets close to the truth, really close to home, and I'll throw out this rather innocuous but loaded statement about, say, her mother. We all do this. That's what this woman at the well was doing with Jesus. She tries to start an argument.

And yet that conversation about her husbands needed to happen, had to happen. This woman eventually gets so excited about Jesus that she runs and tells the rest of the town. Note that she was probably returning to people who had shunned her, talked about her, for many years. "Come see a man who told me everything I've ever done!" Sounds like a carnival sideshow. Now don't you reckon *that* invitation raised a few eyebrows with her neighbors?

For the first time in a long while, this woman had been accepted, all of her, regardless of her past. "Come see this guy who loves me, *even me*, in spite of everything I've ever done!" Jesus meets us all at the well, the font where all pretending, all disguise, is finally stripped away. And he may very well ask us each different questions. We may not have had five husbands and a live-in, but there's a good chance that most of us have had many secret lovers, false gods, that lure us away from the true God.

So imagine yourself sitting with Jesus at a well. He turns and asks each of us about our little faith adulteries, our secret trysts. He might say to one of us, "Go, bring me your bank book and come back and show me how you've been spending your money to help the poor." He might say to someone else, "Come, show me where you go on Sunday mornings that is so much more important than church." And yet to another: "Please help me understand why you're so busy that I haven't heard from you in prayer for a while." Or maybe: "Go ahead, tell me about that event that happened so long ago, that story that's eating you alive from the inside out." What would Jesus ask of *you* by that well?

I find it interesting that the woman in this story is never named. That, I think, is absolutely intentional. For this story is not only about somebody's infidelity long ago. It's also about your infidelity and mine. The other "husbands," the other gods we all have that take the place of Jesus and block full-blown conversion.

Jesus does not confront this unnamed woman in order to condemn or embarrass her. He confronts this woman in order to save her. She needed to die to a past that was killing her—a past that needed to be cleansed, forgiven, buried, drowned, so that new life could come. This is the vocabulary of baptism.

o o o

They met at a well about noon, the same hour authorities would later string him up. She came for water, parched. He came for her. But not any old way, certainly not on her own terms, but fully, totally, maybe even confrontationally, in ways that made her squirm (that today seem utterly shocking to us). And very slowly, certainly not all at once, she realized what she was truly thirsty for—Him.

"Those who drink of the water that I will give them will never be thirsty."

Think of it. He told her everything she had ever done.

Everything.

For Reflection and Discussion

- *Try to recall someone who told you something true about yourself that you really didn't want to hear, a truth that wound up being helpful and even liberating.*

- *How willing are you to allow Jesus into the secret (even shameful) areas of your past?*

- *You might remember the smug, judgmental nature of "The Church Lady" on Saturday Night Live. But consider another angle. What if we need someone like Jesus to enter into our past to share and thereby heal our darkness?*

If You'd Been Here

JOHN 11:1-44

AT THE BEGINNING OF this long, intriguing story about Lazarus' sickness and demise, Jesus says: "This illness does not lead to death." It's a rather strange thing for Jesus to say with such confidence and assurance since his good pal Lazarus, presumably a family friend, does indeed certifiably croak. But Jesus seems rather cool and a bit detached when he first learns about his friend's illness. "Nothing to worry about here," says Jesus. "Don't sweat it," says our Lord. "Merely a chest cold."

This illness does not lead to death. Well, pardon me, Lord, but Lazarus your good buddy and old friend does indeed die in this story. I know you brought him back to life later on and I don't mean to be rude or anything, but talk about a classic misdiagnosis. This illness *did* lead to death. That was no Halloween costume Lazarus wore for fun during those several days wrapped up in the tomb there.

Let's say you're in a hospital, visiting a family member or maybe a dear friend. You're heading for the elevator to go home, understandably worried, and you bump into a doctor who seems to be all smiles. With warm jocularity and comforting reassurance, the doctor promises full and speedy recovery—nothing to worry about. But as it turns out, there was plenty to worry about. Would you be a bit peeved with that doctor? I'd say you would.

This illness does not lead to death. Given what we know about the demise of Lazarus, we have to wonder about this promise of Jesus. What did he mean by that? Did he just blow the prognosis and underestimate the tenacity of his friend's virus? Or is there something more going on here? (There's *always* more going on in a Bible story than meets the eye, by the way, but for just a moment let's stick with the possibility that Jesus is an underachiever.)

"This is nothing to worry about," says Jesus. "Everything's under control." And then he stays put "two days longer in the place where he was" (11:6). Not only that, when Jesus finally does arrive on the scene, Lazarus has been in the tomb "four days" (11:17). It's a kindly stretch to say that Jesus takes his sweet time responding to this situation. Just to bring this closer to home, let's say he was on vacation and had two days remaining on his time-share. He deserves a break after all, right? We cannot say he's "only" human, but he was that too, say our creeds. Did he just blow this one?

Suppose I'm at the beach one week and get a message that a saint of our congregation is dying. It's Monday. The fish are biting, the weather is just about perfect, and the rental deposit on the house cannot be recovered. Pastor Paul, my affable colleague, is on a Global Mission trip to Papua New Guinea and cannot respond, so that leaves me. And what do I do? Well, I decide to pray for that church member from a distance. Don't worry. Prayer travels over the miles, doesn't it? When I return home that Saturday, I discover that our dear friend had a turn for the worse, and not only that, the funeral has already occurred. And so here's the question: Would people be happy about my absence? Would the biting fish be a good excuse? No, on both counts; you know that wouldn't fly. I would have some explaining to do.

And I would never pretend to be Jesus, of course, but he's also got some explaining to do when the two sisters of Lazarus see him ambling casually into town after the funeral is over and after everybody's gone home, having had their fill of fried chicken and potato salad at the wake. Both sisters say the same thing. And although we don't know the inflection in their voices, to be charitable let's say the tone was rather terse. Martha and Mary, in turn, hustle out of the house in a huff and say, with clenched teeth, "If you had been here, my brother would not have died." What they really wanted to say was this: "If you'd gotten off your ass, Jesus, Lazarus would still be around."

I think we should pay attention when people talk back sassily to Jesus. It doesn't happen very often in the gospels, but in this story it happens twice and it's instructive that Jesus takes it. He doesn't threaten to turn the sisters into a pillar of salt or anything. We should pay attention to this bold sisterly challenge because their voices on that road echo the voices in our hearts. If anyone claims that they've never once wondered about the absence of Jesus, I'd say they weren't telling the whole truth. If you've ever been through an agonizing and untimely death with someone, I'd say you may have hurled some version of Martha and Mary's accusation at Jesus: "Lord, if you had been here . . . Where were you, Lord?" And not far behind that: *Where are you?* If Jesus has it in him to heal our loved ones—if he walked on water, and fed five thousand—why this seeming absence?

Some friends of the family of Lazarus speak for all of us when they ask with utter candor: "Could not he who opened the eyes of the blind man have kept this man from dying?" (11:37). Numerous versions of the question are asked in emergency rooms and cancer wards across the country. I don't think we should try and sweep the question away too quickly. "If you'd been here Jesus, this would not have happened. Where were you?" *If only you'd been here.* That's our question, and pretty often at that if we're honest.

Because this story ends on a happy note, with Lazarus coming forth and embracing his sisters, many tend to focus on that end result. Many use this story to say something like this: "This life may seem like one big cemetery, but there will come a day way out in the future when God will call our names and we will rise to live with him forever in heaven." And please don't get me wrong. I believe that. And I've certainly preached that. But there is more going on here than future promise alone.

Jesus looks at Martha on that road and says, "I *am* the resurrection and the life." The present tense here is noteworthy and important for me. Jesus does not say, "I *will* offer resurrection for you some day if you live the right life." He says instead that resurrection can happen now. "I *am* that reality, right now." The more I read this story the more I'm reminded that Christianity and following Jesus is not just some holy inoculation to protect us from the pain of death one day. It's easy to reduce Christianity to a fallback position, some holy rabbit's foot. "Maybe," the logic goes, "I'd better believe in Jesus just in case." If truth were told, I suspect many people, even many church members, hold such a theological view: Jesus as insurance for the future.

But these sisters on that road were holding out for something more. "If you had been here . . ." Sometimes that is our honest accusation. My gut response is that the accusation is grounded in a longing to know Jesus in the here and now, in the midst of life's absurdities and not just in the shadowy future.

Mary Roach speaks the truth when she writes: "Being dead is absurd. It's the silliest situation you'll find yourself in. Your limbs are floppy and uncooperative. Your mouth hangs open. Being dead is unsightly and stinky and embarrassing, and there's not a damn thing to be done about it."[34] One large purpose of the Christian life (and one primary function of the church year) is to rub our noses in death with such frequency and intentionality that we are finally liberated from its paralyzing power over us. Lent invites us to look at the cross squarely and not turn away.

I do not know why people die prematurely and unfairly. And anyone who says they do know is lying. Jesus never claims to protect and shield us from dying. We do know from the details of this story that Jesus is "greatly disturbed" as he approaches the tomb of his friend. The word in the Greek is actually "anger." Jesus is angry, ticked off at death; and famously, he weeps over it.

But Jesus will not be jerked around by death. He will not scurry around according to death's timetable. He takes his time arriving to the cemetery. He talks back to death. He walks straight into a tomb and calls forth life. He will soon walk into his own tomb, only days down the road. Jerusalem, we're told, is only two miles away (11:18). In short, he knows that there are worse things than death itself. And what could that be? Worse, according to Jesus, is our great fear of dying.

This story exposes and names our deepest, most unspoken thoughts about Jesus. "Where were you? If only you'd been here." Let's be honest. Jesus doesn't protect us from death. That is really not what this story is finally about, that everything will turn out okay in the end. "Hang in there, dear sisters on the road. A better day's coming." And all that. No. This story is about courage; so claiming the truth of the resurrection that we carry it with us in the present, into the tombs and darkness of this life.

Jesus looked at Martha and said, "I *am* the resurrection and the life." He looks at us still on all the roads we travel. He looks and asks:

"Do you believe this?"

For Reflection and Discussion

- *Reflect upon this sentence from the essay: "One large purpose of the Christian life (and one primary function of the church year) is to rub our noses in death with such frequency and intentionality that we are finally liberated from its paralyzing power over us."*

- *Do you agree that our great fear of dying is often worse that death itself? Why or why not?*

- *How do you feel about the Jesus in this story who seems to take his sweet time arriving at the tomb of Lazarus?*

8

Unmitigated All

JOHN 12:20-33

IN 1961 NOVELIST PETER De Vries published what became his most famous book, *The Blood of the Lamb.* The main character of the novel, Don Wanderhope, is aptly named. Like many of us, his hope wanders. He loses his faith early in life, regains it for a period of time, and then is thrown into another faith crisis when his young daughter, Carol, is diagnosed with leukemia. I know of few other novels that deal so honestly with the torturous interplay between faith and suffering.

One day Don Wanderhope hears some good news about his daughter's condition. She may live longer than expected. So to celebrate this news, Don purchases a cake to take to the cancer ward but first stops by a local church and prays this prayer: "Give us a year. We will spend it as we have the last, missing nothing. We will mark the dance of every hour between the snowdrop and the snow: crocus to tulip to violet to iris to rose." In the book, the prayer is much longer than this and pledges to notice daily what largely goes unnoticed. A father walks briskly to the hospital to celebrate.

The good news, however, doesn't last long. Carol contracts an infection from the lowered blood counts brought on by her new medication. She will not live through the night. Don Wanderhope leaves the hospital in absolute despair, walks by the church, and remembers the cake he has left on the front pew. Standing now outside on the sanctuary steps, balancing the cake in one hand, he looks up at a large crucifix of Jesus who hangs silently over the doorway.

> It was miracle enough that the pastry should reach its target at all, at that height from the sidewalk. The more so that it should land squarely, just beneath the crown of thorns. Then through scalded eyes I seemed to see the hands free themselves of the nails and move slowly toward the soiled face. Very slowly, very deliberately, with infinite patience, the icing was wiped from the eyes and flung away. I could see it fall in clumps to the porch steps. Then the cheeks were wiped down with the same sense of grave and gentle ritual, with all the kind sobriety of one whose voice could be heard saying, "Suffer the little children to come unto me, for of such is the kingdom of heaven."[35]

There are passages in the Bible that suggest a Great Judgment based upon our behavior, our beliefs, and our faithful allegiance to Jesus. I think of the parable of the Ten Bridesmaids where half are left out in the cold, short on oil, and told by the Bridegroom: "I do not know you." I think of the parable of the Sheep and Goats that describes a great separation of people by the Son of Man when he comes in his glory. And there are other passages I could quote. Our creeds assume a future judgment.

But there are other passages (not a few in number) that seem to suggest a different twist to this judgment. One is from the gospel of John. Greeks, definite outsiders, arrive at the Passover festival. Greeks and Jews didn't hang out together. But there is something about their presence at this festival that sets in motion the events that lead to Jesus' death and resurrection. Throughout this gospel, Jesus has told people "it's not my hour." Not now. Not yet. Not the right time. Outsiders appear and Jesus says, "Okay people, the hour has come" (12:23). The balance of this gospel describes the upper room, arrest, crucifixion, and rising. There is something about these outsiders appearing before Jesus that sets all of this in motion. Strange.

Not only that, but before these events get underway in earnest, Jesus says something that may rattle our theological Scrabble boards just a bit. He says, "And I, when I am lifted up from the earth, will draw all people to myself." Not some. Not just a few. *All.* Everybody. The Greek word for "draw" in this verse is more approximately rendered "drag." The idea here (whether you buy it or not) is that the love of the cross is so powerful and so compelling that people are drawn into the kingdom, dragged into the family, somehow, some way, even against their will. I suspect this idea might just unnerve more than a few Christian sensibilities, but here it is in the Bible.

In C. S. Lewis's book *The Great Divorce*, there is a celestial bus that anybody can board. You get on the bus and it takes you to heaven. Of course it's a wonderful place, but some people prefer earth over heaven so the bus keeps making round trips back to earth to let people off there. Nobody is forced to stay. This verse from John goes a step further than C. S. Lewis. Jesus' love is so compelling that all are eventually on the bus, and no one is left behind.

Now I know what you're thinking. What about Saddam Hussein and Osama bin Laden and Timothy McVeigh and other obvious villains? Surely they will fry. What about somebody like Don Wanderhope who in anger throws a cake straight into the face of Jesus and seems to completely lose his faith? What about my friend Andy who has been an atheist for the twenty-five years I've known him, who once wrote me a letter that began, "Dear Frank: Answer these questions. Answer everything in here, damn it. Answer according to yourself and your religion. What do you mean by God? What is your God? Define God. Christians see God's work in the world selectively," he wrote, "and see God in the Bible selectively. Is your God only in sunsets and curly-headed babies? God must be more consistent. If he chooses not to share himself with us, and not to explain himself, I choose not to respect him." That letter went on for fourteen pages. Will Andy, one of the most compassionate people I know, need to make a hasty conversion some day before he dies in order to be included by Christ? Or is he lost?

I once overheard a Christian respond indignantly to these verses upon considering the wide net described here in John and the utter scandal of Jesus drawing all people towards himself through the cross. "I've lived right all my life," he said, "gone to church every Sunday, never once cheated on my wife or my income taxes . . . there's got to be a hell for people who haven't lived this way!"

He had a point, you know. Christians, however, must be very careful in drawing a line of righteousness between ourselves and other people—even people who seem far beyond the limits of God's love; for God is judge and we are not. For this we can be daily grateful.

In many ways Holy Communion is a dress rehearsal for the life that is to come—a dress rehearsal where sinners of all stripes will be gathered for the great and glorious feast, aggressively drawn together by the God of love. Who knows who will be there? Who knows who will arrive among us any Sunday morning?

This much is true: any goodness we have in us is a reflection of Christ, not our own self-made purity. And if that is true, then perhaps we should loosen up a bit and let God be God. If Jesus wishes to draw all people to himself, then who are we to stand in his way?

From the world's perspective, there is surely a great deal of difference between believers like us and the great global villains. From God's perspective, however, I'm not so sure about that. From God's vantage point, looking out at the world from the height of a cross, we are all greatly loved. All—whether we have a strong faith, a "wandering hope," or have rejected Jesus altogether. We are all greatly loved.

The arms of Christ outstretched reach infinitely further than we can ever imagine.

For Reflection and Discussion

- *How do you feel about the idea of universal salvation? The idea that (somehow, some way) all of humanity will be saved and transformed by God?*

- *"God is judge and we are not." List several reasons we can be grateful for this creedal truth.*

- *Holy Communion is essentially about a "community" of sinners in search of grace. At your next Lord's Supper, envision Jesus as one who draws an astonishing variety of people into communion with one another.*

9

Straddling Two Worlds

MATTHEW 21:1-11

WHEN OUR KIDS were very small, we had a picture book they never tired of viewing. Each set of facing pages was a fairly normal-looking scene—a barnyard, a school playground, a day at the beach. But in each scene a few things were out of place or abnormally illustrated, a little out of whack. The fun was in locating those things and saying things like: *"No,* a bear doesn't have wings, daddy." Or: *"No,* sharks don't play volleyball." Or: *"No,* teachers never climb flagpoles." (That's true for teachers on most days anyway.) The idea was to look at a rather normal panorama and find what did not fit—a brainteaser for little tykes.

Every three years we hear Matthew's version of Palm Sunday and I always have to wonder: Does anybody ever notice how strange this particular version of this old story (known by heart by many) really is? If an artist were to draw the scene exactly as Matthew tells it, you'd notice right away. But Palm Sunday is like the stable in Bethlehem in some ways; the details are so firmly etched in our minds—the waving palms, the excited crowd, the plodding burro—that we might miss Matthew's artistic touches.

And so if we look really hard and play the game my children loved (*What's Wrong with This Picture?*) then we might just notice that Jesus is riding two animals into Jerusalem and not just one. Don't ask me how he does it. Maybe in those lost years between ages twelve and thirty he ran away to the circus for a few months and tried his hand at trick-riding, I don't know.

But Matthew spends a good percentage of his version of this story driving home the presence of two beasts of burden: a donkey *and* a colt. Two were untied, two were brought, and two had cloaks placed upon their backs. The pronoun "them" (describing this braying, equine pair) is used *six times* in three verses. And somehow, Jesus (I'm quoting from verse 7 here) "sat on them." Please add this amazing, trick-riding feat to our Lord's list of lesser-known miracles.

Perhaps you already know that Matthew, who loves to quote from the Good Book throughout his gospel, had his Bible open to a passage from the prophet Zechariah (9:9). And old Zach, in good prophetic and poetic style, describes a single animal with two different Hebrew words. But Matthew, wanting to be faithful to his sources, mistakenly sees two animals in the fulfillment of that old prophecy and, by golly, two will appear in his version of the parade. I'm sure you can see how this line of thinking may make a scriptural fundamentalist rather nervous.

But let's say that Jesus really does ride into the city on two animals. He walked on water and he can manage this. Maybe he stands and straddles these two donkeys with a foot on either saddle, ready for *Rawhide*. Head 'em up, move 'em out. I rather like this image because the very next story (without a breath or verse's pause between them) is the cleansing of the temple—where Jesus knocks over tables, drives out money changers, and raises "h-e-double-toothpicks" with the religious establishment. Some versions of this story include a bullwhip in the hands of Jesus, which nicely complements his rollicking ride into town on the two beasts. So okay, maybe there *were* two donkeys. Fine.

But maybe Matthew knew exactly what he was doing, and maybe more is going on here than an early biblical brainteaser. For me, Jesus' ride into town on two animals provides a wonderful metaphor for his entire ministry. Just as Jesus seems to straddle two donkeys, he also straddles two worlds. *One foot* is squarely planted on this earth as he experiences life and the variety of human emotions, and *another foot* is planted in a kingdom that often seems so very alien to what we experience here on earth—a kingdom of peace and forgiveness, a kingdom of love and acceptance, where enemies become friends, and all will dine together in a great banquet of grace. Some refer to Jesus' disciples as "resident aliens" for this reason as we struggle to live in two worlds. Jesus' entire ministry straddles these two realities. And so bank on this: when the earthly kingdom and the heavenly kingdom rub up against each other with the frequency and creativity lived out by Jesus, sparks will fly, friction.

Jesus so firmly stood with one foot in either place. Something had to give. And so his crucifixion should not really surprise us. A cross is ultimately in the cards for anyone who tries to live out the implications of our Lord's famous prayer: "Thy kingdom come, thy will be done on earth as it is in heaven." *On earth*. Think hard about these words the next time you pray them before Holy Communion. Following Jesus will mean living with a foot in either place. We will need Christ's body and blood to have any hope of living this way because following Jesus may very well require our bodies, our blood—our very lives. *Authentic Christians live in two worlds*. If you don't feel the tension in living such a theological posture, it may be that you've been swallowed by this one. There's a bit of Jonah in us all.

○ ○ ○

A few months back I rode in the lead car with one of our congregation members, Howard, who works for the local funeral home. We were riding from the church to a cemetery for an interment and had several miles to travel, so I said, "Howard, tell me an odd story that's occurred in your line of work as of late." In recent years at the conclusion of graveside funeral services, families occasionally choose to release a dove—as a symbol of peace, a symbol of resurrection and new life, a symbol that the soul of the departed loved one is now ascending toward the clouds with God (even though a traditional understanding of the "resurrection of the body"[36] knows better). Maybe you've seen this avian ascension at a funeral. Howard told me that at the end of a recent service the family released the dove and watched the beautiful bird make several soaring sweeps around the cemetery as someone patiently explained the symbolism. On the dove's second tour of the cemetery, in full view of the mourning family, a hawk shot out of the surrounding trees, grabbed the dove in its talons, and flew away for a late lunch. The raptor had been watching and waiting in the woods. There was an audible gasp from the ground. A funeral home worker was heard to whisper, "You know, we're never doing *that* again."

The beautiful dove, the gentle spirit of Jesus, will be grabbed in the talons of this world every time. The crowd, as you know, turns ugly. His captors and tormentors will wait in the shadows until the opportune time. Jesus' crucifixion should not surprise us, nor should we expect instant immunity from suffering and violence as his followers, as resident aliens. How shall we live as Christians in light of these realities?

Maybe straddling two donkeys is exactly the image we need. Such an image reminds us that Jesus and all authentic followers of Jesus straddle two worlds—this world that we love, this world that both dazzles and blinds, but also another world from which we receive our ultimate marching orders. Two worlds.

In Matthew's version of Palm Sunday, we may be tempted to ask: What's wrong with this picture? What's out of place here? But it may be that this odd two-donkey parade simply helps readjust our focus. Which world is the real world? And which world will most define our days?

"Thy kingdom come," we pray, "on earth as it is in heaven."

For Reflection and Discussion

- *What does this story say to you about how the Bible came to be?*

- *In your early life as a disciple, where have you seen "sparks fly" as the kingdoms of earth and heaven create friction between one another?*

- *How do you understand this famous petition from the Lord's Prayer: "Thy kingdom come, thy will be done, on earth as it is in heaven"?*

EASTER

Easter

On a Friday many murky centuries ago, Jesus was crucified between two criminals. He died of blood loss and, more accurately say most scholars, asphyxiation. On Sunday morning he's up and around and stands among frightened disciples who gather that evening behind closed doors (John 20:19-23). Here's a detail from the story that has always been a bit baffling to me: "Peace be with you," says the once-dead Jesus. "After he said this, he showed them his hands and his side." Not even a howdy-do escapes his mouth before he shows those disciples his scars, his wounds.

You'd think Jesus would do a better job of teaching the disciples what the Easter life is all about, the real benefits of resurrection. You know, the "streets paved with gold"—those benefits. But the tomb is hardly cold when Jesus appears, hikes up his shirt, shows the guys exactly where the spear pierced his side, and gives a palms-up tour of the nail damage. "Peace be with you, but now take a gander at my wounds." The transition is so sudden in the text that one wonders if the Easter peace brought by Jesus is somehow connected to the bold parading of his scars.

This scene is not what many Christians of my acquaintance have come to expect from Easter. For them, Easter is one big carefree entrance into a theological nirvana of sorts that's a lot like that song, "The Big Rock Candy Mountain." According to much popular Christianity, Easter and the cross have nothing to do with one another. One of the surprising truths for Easter Christians is that the peace of Christ is intimately connected to the wounds of Christ. We worship the crucified *and* risen Lord, separating those words at our peril.

The Easter season intends to bring our own wounds into the light of Christ's promise. Our agonies are given new perspective by the One who makes "all things new" (Revelation 21:5).

THEN THEY remembered HIS words, and returning from THE TOMB, THEY TOLD ALL THIS TO THE eLeven and TO ALL THE rest. (LUKE 24:8-9)

1

Cemetery Amnesia

LUKE 24:1-12

E. B. WHITE, author of *Charlotte's Web*, once watched his wife Katharine plant flower bulbs in her garden just before she died, in the last autumn of her life. They both knew she was dying. Even so, he was amused at the sight of the woman he loved still taking spade to soil. He wrote: "There was something comical yet touching in her bedraggled appearance . . . the small hunched-over figure, her studied absorption in the implausible notion that there would be yet another spring, oblivious to the ending of her own days, which she knew perfectly well was near at hand, sitting there with her detailed chart under those dark skies in dying October, calmly plotting the resurrection."

Have you ever known people like Katharine White? People who were coming right up to the reality of death, even knew it was right around the corner, but never once complained, never panicked, but lived their last days as if—well, as if life would never end? There is a certain peace about such people that is enviable. My good friend, Bill, died of a brain tumor after an excruciating year of surgery and failed treatments. His wife told me after the funeral that he never once complained during the illness or wondered about the fairness of it all, not even privately to her. How does one sit there with a detailed flower chart under the dark skies of your last October? What wisdom allows a person to stare down death in such a way?

One of my favorite cartoonists is a very offbeat guy named John Callahan. He also happens to be a quadriplegic, paralyzed from a car accident when he was a young man. Of all his cartoons, my favorite shows Jesus hanging on a cross. But Jesus' head isn't bowed. Instead, Jesus is grinning; in fact, he's absolutely beaming. Above his head is tacked the traditional placard. But it doesn't say, INRI, the famous Latin acronym for "Jesus of Nazareth, King of the Jews." In its place is a sign that reads: TGIF. *Thank God It's Friday.* Jesus himself can laugh at that I suspect. But I'm interested in a question behind the cartoon. And it's really a question about resurrection. How does John Callahan, his life as good as over after his car accident, now find such joy and humor in what he does? What inner wisdom allows a person to thumb his nose at death in such a liberating way? What releases people from their tombs on this side of the grave?

All of us are occasionally "entombed" by something. Easter faith ebbs and flows. Events in this life shake us. Almost every member of any church I've ever served has either experienced (or is coming through) an event in their lives that seems utterly paralyzing, where life seems all but over. It isn't, of course, according to Jesus, but how do we come to that confident moment where the resurrection becomes the ultimate reality in our lives, even in the midst of actual death or what feels a whole lot like it? There is a big difference between saying that "Christ is risen!" on Easter Sunday with a joyful throng, and allowing that resurrection reality to permeate and define our days.

Some women come to a tomb on that Sunday so long ago. A careful reader will notice that these grave-checkers are not named until 75 percent of this Easter story is told. Luke uses the collective pronoun "they" a total of eight times before finally bothering to identify the women in verse 10. This is undoubtedly Luke's way of pulling us into the story. So when you see the word "they" in these verses, just insert your own name, or yours and the name of a friend or two who may be trapped these days in a tomb-like existence. See if the drama doesn't come alive in a new way.

For all the joy that Easter morning holds for Christians, it's important to linger at the tomb just a bit and recall how observant Jewish people marked death—quite a contrast to how modern people often want to "get through it" as quickly as possible. "Among observant Jews," reports my source, "those closest to the deceased observe *shiva* for seven days following the death. During *shiva* one does not work, bathe, put on shoes, engage in intercourse, read Torah, or have one's hair cut. The mourners are to behave as though they themselves had died."[37] A month-long period follows that first week and then a tempered year of mourning after that first month. This old invitation to ritually mark an extended period of grief is undoubtedly what these women were beginning that first Easter morning—a healthy way to deal with death. (I've encountered more than one inebriated mourner, lubricating their great sadness in the hours just following the death of a loved one; to face grief head-on requires immense courage.)

But something happens to interrupt all this. And please keep Katharine White (who planted those autumn flower bulbs) and John Callahan (the quadriplegic) in mind as you consider this interruption—not to mention your own name and the names of others I invited you to insert into the story a moment ago. "*We* came to the tomb, *we* found the stone rolled away, *we* were terrified." It doesn't take a lot of imagination to name our own tombs as we reflect upon the tomb of Jesus.

But something happens. Something happens to interrupt the *shiva*, the mourning, the smothering grief. What is that something? And here's a hint: it's not as obvious as you may think.

Two dazzling men suddenly appear. I love these guys. They scare the bee-jeebies out of these women. But they are the key to unlocking Easter. Please notice how they relate to these women, full of sorrow, who have come to the cemetery to begin their *shiva*. Here's what you'd expect from angels, if that's what they are: you'd expect a little comfort, a few "fear nots" thrown around, an arm around somebody's shoulder. "There, there," they might say. But no, here's what these men of manners offer: "What the heck are you doing here looking for your friend among dead people? Well, he's not here! Sorry, you just missed him." Few would ever be so bold with grieving people bringing flowers to a grave. Remember: all of this compassionate counsel occurs in the middle of a tomb. Let that soak in. (An aside: it's been suggested that a baptismal font is nothing more than an empty tomb filled with water. Ponder that: death and birth are potentially close cousins.)

But there's more. We're approaching the key to this Easter story and the key to our own serenity as we kneel in the dirt in the dark days of our own future dying October. The dazzling men say, "*Remember, remember how he told you . . . that the Son of Man must be handed over to sinners, and be crucified, and on the third day rise again.*" Remember all that. In the middle of that tomb the women are encouraged to recall the very words that Jesus once shared with them. *In the middle of that tomb*, they are urged to make his words present.

Verse 8 reports: "Then." *Then.* It's the most important word in the entire story. "*Then* they remembered his words." At that moment, in the middle of that cemetery, they recalled the words of Jesus and sprang forth from the tomb. *Easter happened then.* The words they recalled—not the emptiness of the space, not the missing body, *but the words*—freed them from the pall of death. They are awakened from their collective amnesia to an Easter existence. They snap out of it. They are re-created through his words.

The Greek word here for "remember" is the same word used every Sunday in the Eucharist: "Do this in *remembrance* of me" over bread and wine. This is not the same as saying, "Let's be sure to remember the life of Abraham Lincoln." At Holy Communion, we are not commemorating a dead hero and recalling his important life once upon a time and long ago. Here, the word "remember" is used another way. This word intends to bring the past into the actual present. When we "remember" Christ in such a way, it is like waking up, or opening your eyes, taking a cold shower. Remembering Jesus not only recalls his past, but also creates our present. Luke says *that* is Easter.

Your tomb: that one you may be mired in right now, down on your knees. Your tomb: your daily dread of the coming future. Your tomb: that paralyzing fear of death that affects how we all live. What part of *you*, known or hidden, needs to be raised from the dead? After all, the real question for Easter is not, "Did it really happen?" The real question is rather: "Is it really happening?"

So how do we talk back to the tombs we all inevitably enter? *How does Easter work?* Well, for starters, it might behoove us to know the words of Jesus. To pore over them as we might handle pearls. To live them as if he is speaking straight to us, because he is. It was his word, we are told, that created the world. His words, then, will create a new people. That, in short, is how Easter happens.

So remember. *Remember.* Here's the secret to planting flower bulbs under a late October sky, or even saying TGIF from your own cross. Here's the real key to living an Easter life:

One verse. The eighth. "Then they remembered his words."

For Reflection and Discussion

- *Recall, if possible, a friend who faced death in a confident, uncomplaining fashion. What abiding truth did you learn from your friend?*

- *In your encounters with the Bible thus far, what particular words of Jesus give you courage to stare down even death?*

- *What difference does it make to you that Jesus' words are not only addressed to people twenty centuries ago, but also directly to us today?*

"were not our hearts burning within us while he was talking to us on the road, while he was opening the scriptures to us?" (Luke 24:32)

2

Seven-Mile Reversal

LUKE 24:13-35

IT'S GETTING DARK, TWI-light. Two men approach the town limits in a slow, shuffling sort of fashion, revealing something more on their minds than a warm bed and a meal. There's something bothering these two. Can you see it?

They look like they've just come from a funeral of a good friend. They keep walking, heads down, occasionally talking in low tones.

Who are these men? Why are they heading this way? One of them goes by Cleopas, the only time he's ever mentioned in the Bible. The other hiker is never named. I am all but invited to walk along. So are you.

Notice something: they are heading *away* from Jerusalem. Miles (seven miles on foot the story reports) now separate these two from their old friends who still wait in the city and dare to hope. As far as I can tell, these two have pretty much given up on their old community of friends; have given up on Jesus; have given up on what would soon become the church. They are slowly walking the other way.

I won't judge them for that. And I won't say I've never been there with them on that road—despondent, without hope. Sometimes it seems that "church" is little more than going through the motions. Faith (a gift, according to Martin Luther) comes and goes. "Lord, I believe, help my unbelief," a worried father once confessed to Jesus.[38] Honest Christians have lots in common with these two men on the road to Emmaus. And walking the other way, away from the community, away from Jerusalem towards the Emmaus of my imagination, is a very real and appealing possibility. Who hasn't thought of chucking church?

They tell the stranger on the road: "We had hoped that he was the one to redeem Israel." *Had hoped*. There are few things more wrenching in this life than hope once cherished, now lost. "Had hoped," they say. Their eyes were wide open now. Jesus was as dead as a doornail. The party's over. Time to head home and be grown-ups about this. Leave the other suckers in Jerusalem, but we prefer a little honesty here. "We *had hoped*. . . ."

In John Updike's novel *In the Beauty of the Lilies*, published in 1996, Clarence Wilmot is the pastor of Fourth Presbyterian Church in Paterson, New Jersey. In the year 1910, Clarence wakes up one morning with an overwhelming feeling of "God's inexorable recession." Clarence has been fighting feelings of doubt for some time since reading a controversial book called *Some Mistakes of Moses*. The book so upsets Pastor Clarence that he finally decides to resign his call and sell encyclopedias door to door. Clarence concludes that he's much more comfortable with facts than speculation, so he sells these books of facts now.

John Updike writes: "Clarence's mind was like a many-legged, wingless insect that had long and tediously been struggling to climb up the walls of a slick-walled porcelain basin; and now a sudden impatient wash of water swept it down into the drain. *There is no God*, Clarence thinks to himself."[39] Updike, who grew up in the Lutheran church, says a lot about our culture's need for getting the facts straight. The facts for those two on the road to Emmaus were quite clear. Jesus was dead. *We had hoped, but...* I'll say it again: there is nothing quite so devastating as hope once cherished, now lost. Better, perhaps, to trust facts only from the get-go.

But fast-forward just a moment to the end of the story. These same two guys, one Cleopas, the other unnamed, walking *away* from Jerusalem, *away* from the community, *away* from church, now race back *towards* all three. First, slowly and hopelessly away, now hastily and hopefully towards. It's dark now, and they decide to hike the seven miles anyway! What kind of news would cause you to walk seven miles in the dark?

What makes these two now return to the community, to church? Is it the sight of Jesus? Surely that had something to do with it. But I think there's a lot more here. The two look at one another and say, "Were not our hearts burning within us while he was talking to us on the road, while he was opening the scriptures to us?" It was not so much the sight of Jesus that brought them to faith. Indeed, their hearts burned before they knew who it was. It was the conversation with the scriptures, the "Holy Heartburn" of hearing the word anew. Their hope in Jesus revives through an encounter with the word. And through the breaking of the bread, their eyes are opened. Right here in this old story is a rationale for a liturgical emphasis on word and sacrament. Hearts burn when the *word* is broken open. Eyes see new things when the *bread* is broken.

People go away from Jerusalem, away from church, lose hope in Jesus, for a variety of reasons. I've watched them go and also experienced the tendency in myself. Primary among the reasons for this loss of hope is a slow abandonment of these two things: in-depth study of the Word and attention to weekly celebration of Holy Communion. This is how Jesus gets into us, gets close to us, rises in us. It's not magic. There's nothing fancy about becoming a dynamic and lively congregation. We feast on scripture. And we feast on Jesus together. Do that faithfully and the Holy Spirit will do the rest.

Words matter. Words form us. "In the beginning was the word." Carefully observe the diet of words upon which you feast. Abandon a serious study of God's word and other words will form you soon enough, capture your heart. This is a hard truth for many modern people who believe that the self is sovereign. "I know what's best for my life." In point of fact, I'm really and truly not born knowing what's best for my life. Christians believe that we become our true selves only by listening to Jesus. We are formed by his words. We feast on his life and slowly see.

Eugene Peterson writes: "Christians do not simply learn or study or use scripture; we assimilate it, take it into our lives in such a way that it gets metabolized into acts of love, cups of cold water, missions into all the world, healing and evangelism and justice in Jesus' name, hands raised in adoration of the Father."[40]

In short, we "eat" the word, serve it up in creative ways, turn it round and around in our lives like a many-faceted jewel, gnaw on it, chew it up, and swallow it into our lives. Along with the Eucharist, the word is a Christian's primary nourishment. Recalling the angel's command to Ezekiel from the introduction ("Eat this scroll"), a regular diet of scripture is a necessity for all those on the Easter journey. We simply get lost without this food.

Jesus catches up with those two guys going away from the community, away from the church. "Goodness and mercy," sings the Psalmist, "shall follow me all the days of my life" (23:6). The Hebrew word for "follow" in this passage is the same word used to describe Pharaoh and his henchmen who "follow" the children of Israel to the Red Sea. This is no idle ambling; Pharaoh is in aggressive pursuit. Jesus is forever tailing us with goodness and mercy. Always close behind, on our heels, no matter where we wander off to. He intends to overtake and catch us.

But please notice that when he does catch up to us, the way of life he offers is not just any old way. Not just any old path leads to Easter. He has given us specific means, old and timeworn paths that lead to open eyes and burning hearts. He has given us Word and Sacrament. We abandon these gifts at our peril, for something else is always waiting to form us, shape us, and take us down a path of our own devising.

Long ago, two followers of Jesus walked along a seven-mile road. In one direction they walked hopelessly and slowly. In the other direction they moved quickly and with purpose. Who knows what the broken bread and the broken-open word can do in your life? I'd say that once Cleopas and his unnamed friend caught their breath back in Jerusalem after those seven miles, they were never the same again.

They had gotten a glimpse of the risen Jesus, and their hearts were burning.

And here's the thing:

They knew how to find him again.

For Reflection and Discussion

- *Has there been a time in your life when you have given up on Jesus? What were the circumstances that led to your rejection?*

- *What kind of news would cause you to walk seven miles in the dark?*

- *If you are new to the church, how has a new diet of word and sacrament changed your understanding of the word "hope"?*

"TOUCH me and see; for a ghost does not have flesh and bones as you see that I have." (Luke 24:39)

3

Body and Soul

LUKE 24:36-43

when our children were very small their first cat died. Cycle was jet black and so named because I found her as a kitten one afternoon on a bicycle trip near Boone, North Carolina, and stuffed her that day right into my handlebar bag with just her little head sticking out. When she died we dug a hole in the backyard, wrapped her tenderly in a pillowcase, and made a marker for her grave. We had a short funeral service for Cycle under a hemlock tree, giving God thanks for all she had meant to us.

The dirt was barely tamped down and the prayers hardly over when our kids got into an argument. They wanted to know where their beloved kitty was at that precise moment. One of the girls said, "She's in heaven." Our son, ever the realist at age 3 said, "No, she's in the gwoun'." He pointed to the dirt. Another finger pointed

157

skyward. "No, in heaven." And so it went, raging on for a few minutes right there beside the grave as one child, then another, passionately declared Cycle's whereabouts. "In heaven," said one. "No, in the gwoun'," insisted the other.

Christians have always wondered and asked about the resurrection life. When will it happen? What will it look like? What will we do there? Even the early church, even those who actually encountered the risen Jesus and told their descendants the earliest stories about those Easter encounters, had their own set of questions when they finally got around to writing the stories down. One Easter story from Luke obviously struggles with a resurrection question that early Christians wondered about.

Jesus appears to disciples who are scared out of their wits. Recognize the source of this fear? Well, they thought Jesus was a ghost, and no Casper the Friendly. Jesus takes quite a bit of time to show these disciples that he's not a spirit, no spook; that he indeed has a body with flesh and bones. "Have you anything here to eat?" asks the risen Jesus. Ghosts don't require broiled sea bass. This is no ghost. By telling this story, which appears nowhere else in the gospels, Luke is addressing a resurrection question that must have piqued the curiosity of many. Namely, "What does a resurrected body look like?"

To be honest, I really have no idea what happens to somebody just after they die. I, of course, believe that resurrection happens; I just don't know *how or when*. But I do feel impelled to share what early Christians meant when they drafted the Apostles' Creed and said, among other things, "I believe in the resurrection of the body."

The resurrected Jesus took special pains to show the disciples that he had a physical body. He wasn't a disembodied, ephemeral spirit; he had flesh and bones. This is not a minor detail of the story. In Jesus' day, most people were shaped by Greek thought. Greeks believed in a certain, well-defined distinction between body and soul. The "immortality of the soul" is the very Greek idea that the soul is the really important part of the person and the body is just a temporary house or shell we happen to occupy until the really good part of you splits off at death and moves on to the happy hunting grounds.

Humans had to put up with the body's inherent urgings, lusts, odors, and upkeep until blessed death. The soul was then free to wander the cosmos like a freed bird seeking total self-actualization. For the Greeks, dying was the ultimate, never-ending beer commercial. Your spry soul bounces on the beach playing eternal volleyball (and other things) with various nubile souls while your worthless shell of a body rots back on earth. At death, your spirit is liberated instantaneously and completely from your body and goes elsewhere. You really don't die at all. You just enter a new spiritual plane. These very Greek ideas are still popular with New Age authors such as Deepak Chopra who says, "Death is ultimately just another transformation, from one configuration of matter and energy to another."[41] Nothing to it, really.

Anyway, that's what the Greeks thought. Spirit was considered "good." Flesh and bodies were seen as "bad." Again, I do not pretend to know what happens exactly when we die, but classic Christian theology definitely parts ways with the "immortality of the soul." Here body and soul are not separate, but completely and eternally united. Author and theologian Frederick Buechner puts this rather bluntly: "The body and soul . . . are as inextricably part and parcel of each other as the leaves and flames that make up a bonfire. When you kick the bucket, you kick it one hundred percent."[42]

When we die, claimed these early Christians, it's not that a soul flutters away into the clouds somewhere while we bury or cremate the body. Body and soul die *together*. There is no such thing as "immortality of the soul" in Christian thought. When we die our whole united being dies. And when we are raised, our whole united being, albeit transformed, is resurrected. This is what the drafters of the creed meant when they said, "I believe in the resurrection *of the body*." Body and soul are eternally united—at birth, death, and always. Don't get hung up on how this happens: what you'll look like in the hereafter, whether or not to cremate, excessive worry about donating your organs to another needy body because you might need them later on. Our God is a creative God and will take care of those concerns.

Our creeds take special pains to tell us that Jesus actually *died*.

That he really and truly croaked. That he was fully human and not just some divine Superman for whom the cross was no real sweat. Do you remember in the *Wizard of Oz* where Dorothy's airborne house lands in Munchkin-land and kills the Wicked Witch of the East? In the movie you see her toes underneath the porch. The little people have lived in such terror of this witch; they need proof that she is "certifiably" dead. So the coroner strolls up in that big black hat of his and sings:

> As Coroner, I must aver,
> > I thoroughly examined her.
> And she's not only *merely* dead;
> > she's really most sincerely dead.[43]

And then the Munchkins go ape.

The early church needed to establish that Jesus was not just "merely" dead, but *dead as a doornail*. In order to certify his humanity, his body *and* soul went to the grave. In order to certify God's power over death, his soul *and* body rose from the grave. "Have you anything here to eat?" Jesus wanted to know. It's a wonderful Easter question.

You may be wondering what in the world all this has to do with Christians twenty centuries removed. Well, plenty. When we say, "I believe in the resurrection of the body," Christians are essentially confessing that the physical things of this world are created to be honored and celebrated. Such a doctrine suggests that Jesus cares about bodies, about human sexuality, about the physical, about ecology and the earth, about how we treat the aging and the newly born and those who lack basic physical needs. This old Easter story suggests that the physical and the spiritual are forever wedded. Matter *matters* to God. Too much Christian theology posits that the earth is just a waiting place, a holding area, until we all get to heaven one day.

Jesus had a body when he rose. He was no ghost. He requested something as normal and material as food. Baptism is always a dunking into both physical and spiritual realms. Body and soul united. What God has joined together let no one put asunder.

For Reflection and Discussion

- *Why do you think it was important for early Christians to affirm resurrection of a body?*

- *Why do you believe "the immortality of the soul" is such a popular idea with so many people?*

- *How might a recovery of this old creedal truth affect the way we care for the earth?*

4

Church Etiquette

ACTS 1:15-26

ONE THING THAT never gets taught in seminary (but probably should be taught) is the fine art of ecclesiastical propriety—what gets mentioned in church and what is better left unsaid. After twenty years of serving as a pastor in various settings, I've noticed with interest those items that are publicly announced and discussed without hesitation. And then I've also noticed how other items make their way around the parish grapevine, but always covertly and in rather hushed tones. Maybe the seminary could call this new course, "The Fine Art of Church Etiquette: When to Speak Up and When to Shut-Up If You Wish to Keep Your Job."

For example, we would certainly want to announce the pregnancy and subsequent birth of a new baby in the parish and ask for prayers for all concerned. It's more difficult, however, to announce the pregnancy of a 17-year-old unmarried teenager who has bravely decided to keep her child despite the odds. It's one thing to joyfully report the news of Bob and Mary's wedding and their blissful honeymoon at Hilton Head, but it's another thing entirely to announce that a couple is breaking up—in fact, we usually don't do that in church even though the couple probably needs our prayers more at that point than ever before. If Johnny makes valedictorian at a local high school, we should certainly praise God for that and honor him with public affirmation. But what if Sally has a drug problem? Do we publicly announce that she's checked into a treatment facility so everyone can pray? Why or why not? Some illnesses are naturals to make it onto the church prayer list; others never appear. Some details are reported, others only whispered about. I'm not really complaining about this; just an observation about parish life. But there's an undeniable line of propriety in every parish—what's acceptable for Sunday morning and what isn't. A question: *Who decides where the line is drawn?*

In the book of Acts, we are given an unusual glimpse of the early church gathered for Sunday worship. There were about 120 of them, all abuzz about the morning's news. Jesus has just ascended into heaven and Pentecost is still a few days away. The church was sort of in this in-between place. One thing they needed to deal with that Sunday morning, requiring the most sensitive and delicate deliberation in constitutional protocol, was the whole matter of Judas the traitor. The church needed new leadership. We learn in this lesson about the mechanics of replacing Judas as one of the twelve. The assembly prays. They call on the name of the Lord. And they cast lots, which basically consisted of writing the two names on stones, placing them in a vessel, and shaking both until one fell out. In effect, they draw straws. They didn't vote, you see. This was not a democracy. The early church radically relied on God to guide them. "Lord, you know everyone's heart, show us which one you've chosen." It might be interesting to elect modern church leaders this way.

What amazes me most, however, is the content of Peter's sermon that Sunday morning. He gets down to the nitty-gritty in a hurry and describes, right out loud, the rather grisly demise of Judas. And please don't think that Peter is moralistically pointing fingers here. You may recall that Peter has his own boatload of shame and guilt that he's carrying around from back in Holy Week when the questions of a servant girl and his own successive denials sent the poor guy into the shadows instead of standing up for Jesus. Judas cannot be the church's convenient whipping boy. There's a little bit of Judas in all of us.

So Peter is not pointing fingers here, but neither is he holding anything back. Peter stands before the congregation that morning; he's made the parish announcements and maybe heard a few prayer requests. Perhaps they sang a hymn or two. And then Peter launches into the sermon. Now if Peter had gone to seminary then maybe he would've learned that you just don't talk about certain subjects in church. Certain things are best whispered about in the parking lot, and to say them out loud in a House of God might make Emily Post flip over in her grave. Some things cannot be uttered in such a holy place if you expect to get out alive.

But Peter didn't go to seminary so he said of Judas, "Now this man acquired a field with the reward of his wickedness; and falling headlong, he burst open in the middle and all his bowels gushed out."[44] My heavens, could Peter not have shown a little pastoral discretion here? Did those 120 people really need that much information? Were mothers and fathers cupping their hands over the ears of their little ones? Or was this sort of honesty and candor a regular part of Sunday morning in the early church, an affirmation that we can bring even the dark spots of our individual and collective histories before the God of new beginnings?

Sunday mornings can often be a rather antiseptic experience in much of America. Certain things we can talk about with much approval and head-nodding. And other things are just politely off-limits. We pray for all sorts of situations and hardly mention others out of fear of embarrassment or plain good taste. Many churches in the south in the 1960s made nary a reference to racial injustice on Sunday mornings. Many churches in Nazi Germany remained strangely silent about the obvious evils occurring all around them. Many churches in this new century pretend that issues of poverty, sexuality, affluence, and environmental degradation are simply not appropriate topics for congregational conversation. You can learn quite a bit about a person, a family, a political leader, or even a congregation by listening closely for what is never mentioned publicly.

Churches can create a conspiracy of silence where everything becomes mannerly, ordered, expected, and above all, *nice*—the southern way to maintain decorum. I think this may be the 11th commandment for those who live below the Mason-Dixon Line—"*Now be nice.*" So survive the hour, remove the tie and makeup at home, but never let your hair down at church. Peter's earthy sharing with his congregation reminds me that we have a long way to go to shake off the taboos of what sort of language is acceptable and unacceptable in church. What really needs to be said on Sunday mornings that we may be afraid to say out loud?

Peter's public conversation about the guts of Judas may just give us enough courage and gumption to spill our own guts in church—to talk openly and honestly about our mission and what we need to do as a church community in Christ's name. We have a guide in these matters, you know. As he hung there that Friday afternoon, one of the soldiers came forward and pierced his side with a spear. Remember what flowed out of those wounds? Blood and water, the very innards of our Lord. We follow a Savior who spilled his guts for us.

It seems that the early church picked up on this sacrificial act as a metaphor for their life together. Nothing could be held back because Jesus held nothing back. All was held in common, even their deepest emotions.

The very gut of the matter.

For Reflection and Discussion

- *Name several types of prayer concerns in your own congregational setting that seem to be spoken with some regularity and also name several things that are never* spoken aloud. What criteria are used to determine what is shared?

· Do you think it was appropriate for Peter to be so honest about Judas in a sermon? Why or why not?

· Reflect upon this sentence from the essay: "You can learn quite a bit about a person, a family, a political leader, or even a congregation by listening closely for what is never mentioned publicly."

AN ANGEL OF THE LORD SAID TO PHILIP, "GET UP AND GO TOWARD THE SOUTH TO THE ROAD THAT GOES DOWN FROM JERUSALEM TO GAZA." (THIS IS A WILDERNESS ROAD.) SO HE GOT UP AND WENT. (ACTS 8:26-27A)

5

Boundary Waters

ACTS 8:26-40

IF YOU HAPPENED TO BE an outsider in the early years of Israel and wanted to be restored to full membership in the community, there were certain liturgical hoops you could jump through and you were welcomed back in. It wasn't easy but certainly possible. For example, if you had leprosy and were seeking reinstatement, you showed yourself to a priest who promptly apprehended two birds. One bird was sliced open and its blood was sprinkled on the patient exactly seven times. The other bird was released as a sign that the disease had left the afflicted. The ex-leper was then required to live outside the camp for a full week. On the seventh day (did you expect any other day?) the person shaved head, beard (if applicable), and eyebrows. Oil was then placed on his or her right earlobe, right thumb, and right big toe—never the left, always the right. The leper was then pronounced "clean" and welcomed back into the community. It's right there in the Bible—Leviticus chapter 14 if you'd like to look it up. Fascinating homecoming ceremony if you ask me.

Other outsiders were not so lucky. They remained outsiders no matter what they did to get in. Let me quote from a little later in Leviticus, chapter 21. These are actually instructions governing the regulations of who could serve as a priest; in other parts of the Old Testament they serve as a "who's who" of folk to be kept at a distance: "For no one who has a blemish shall draw near, one who is blind or lame, or one who has a mutilated face or limb too long, or one who has a broken foot or a broken hand, or a hunchback, or a dwarf, or a man with a blemish in his eyes or an itching disease or scabs or crushed testicles" (21:18-20).

Now you might praise God that religious communities no longer keep such lists. But my point in dabbling in our liturgical past is to say that we most certainly do—keep lists, that is. There is somebody walking around in your hometown community whose past or very person would make you rather nervous if an usher were to hand them a bulletin and sit them down right beside you for the duration of a worship service. All of us draw the line in different places, but we all draw it somewhere. No matter what your church sign might say ("Everyone Welcome," for example), who is honestly not welcome and why? That, I daresay, would be a revealing and theologically constructive conversation.

I'm assuming this eunuch mentioned here in Acts, a black, Ethiopian outsider, was not welcome after he rode the four hundred miles to Jerusalem and tried to get in for worship. He was searching for God, hungry for some word from the Lord, but this blemished foreigner was surely turned away. The Bible clearly says he isn't welcome in Deuteronomy 23:1—"No one whose testicles are crushed or whose penis is cut off shall be admitted to the assembly of the Lord." My confirmation students gleefully enjoy hearing my explanation of what a eunuch actually is. This much is certain: his kind were not welcome in worship, according to scripture. I don't know how they checked this sort of thing at the door, but it's as plain as day, right there in black and white: a eunuch had no place in God's family.

Now here's where the story gets interesting. The Bible clearly says this blemished man from the other side of the world is not welcome in God's house. He starts to head home to Africa, head buried in the Bible, foraging around in scripture, flipping through the pages, desperately seeking his name, his lineage, a home. This man is a foreign, black, sexually ambiguous outsider who has likely just been rejected in Jerusalem. According to the Bible, eunuchs are not welcome, and now he's heading home.

Meanwhile, Philip (not the apostle, but another Philip) receives instructions from "an angel of the Lord." We learn elsewhere in Acts that Philip was father to "four unmarried daughters who had the gift of prophecy" (21:9), and I can only imagine the domestic dynamic of this interesting family arrangement. Anyway, this angel instructs Philip to go to a deserted road and the text says it all: *so he got up and went.* He got up and went! Maybe he needed a break from the four unmarried daughters and was more than willing to "get up and go" but this strikes me as exactly the sort of thing I wouldn't do; a little too impetuous, spontaneous. But Philip doesn't think twice about the boundaries he is crossing or about the man he eventually plops down beside in that pew (I mean chariot) on that deserted road in the middle of nowhere.

Time out here for a short commercial break concerning that most valuable of Bible study tools, the gift of *context*. Do you recall what surrounds this strange story of a blemished man in the book of Acts? Just before and after? Aren't you dying to know? In this same chapter, Philip has just baptized a batch of sorry Samaritans, the quintessential Jewish outsiders. And just one chapter later, that notorious hater of Christians is baptized and converted: Saul who becomes St. Paul. And one chapter after that, Cornelius the Gentile and his whole house are baptized. A whole passel of outsiders surrounds this story of a blemished eunuch. Something weird is indeed happening on that Wilderness Road with this suspicious African who's not supposed to be allowed entrance into God's family. But beyond that, there's a whole lot of weirdness going on here in Acts. The church in these old stories is coloring outside the lines. I'm sure that the leaders back at First Jerusalem Church were a little nervous about these baptisms. Going purely by the book, purely by tradition, solely by what had come before, that foreign, blemished, black outsider would be urged to ride on back home to Africa. And good riddance; he just didn't fit in.

But the Holy Spirit has other plans. And please note that these plans of the Spirit are often so very different from our own. It's so much more comfortable to worship and mingle with people who are mostly alike—people with the same politics, same racial background, same sexual orientation, and similar theological convictions. Some experts in evangelism circles maintain that churches won't grow unless members reach out to others exactly like them—even call this the "Homogenous Unit Principle." But the Spirit will not sit still long enough to allow a homogenous church. The Spirit continually grafts outsiders into the Body of Christ; people who don't seem to fit anywhere.

"What is to prevent me from being baptized?" the outsider asks. Well, come to think of it, there was *a lot* to prevent the baptism from happening, ample biblical warrant for keeping him out. But the Spirit had other plans.

In the state of Minnesota, there is a place called the Boundary Waters—beautiful wilderness and hundreds of natural lakes near the Canadian border. I canoed and camped there many years ago with my wife Cindy when she was seven months pregnant with our first child. She sat up in the bow with a pillow, like a queen. I remember gliding over the waters called Boundary, thinking of my family's future; apprehensive, yet knowing we were supported and kept afloat by another family born in waters that obliterate boundaries—the family known as church.

Read the Bible closely and you'll discover that the Spirit's music is not something humans are able to create, compose, contain, or hinder. The Spirit is always ahead of us—always creating new openings, new passageways. We do not compose this music or try to contain and preserve it for the centuries. Instead, we are forever trying to keep up with the Spirit's music, to try and stay on key, bounding down a desert road with Philip in a rickety chariot and plunging into uncharted waters. What a strange symphony this is.

If Christ is alive, as we profess, and not dead back in the first century, there's at least as much potential for heresy in ignoring the future as there is in ignoring the past. "On the day when I can no longer believe in the resurrection," says writer Garret Keizer, "I shall no longer be able to follow Christ. It's not that I require a reward after death," he says, "it's just that I refuse to have a dead guy running my life."[45] Jesus is no dead guy.

If Jesus is indeed alive, if the Spirit is active in the world, isn't it possible that new directions are in the offing for congregations like yours and mine? It wasn't supposed to happen. A bunch of Samaritans are baptized. A murderous bounty hunter like Saul is converted. A foreign outsider is grafted into a family that became the largest family in the world.

Who authorized these things? Nobody but the Spirit of the living Lord.

An Easter question always remains for the choir of Christ: *Are we in tune or off key?*

For Reflection and Discussion

- *How has the popular church-sign "Everyone Welcome" been lived out or limited in congregations of your acquaintance?*

- *How do you feel about certain Bible stories (this one, for example) contradicting or overturning previous biblical laws?*

- *How do we begin to judge and evaluate the relative power and authority of such contradictory texts?*

6

Raising Gazelle

ACTS 9:36-43

In my former parish in Virginia there was an older woman named Evelyn, beloved by all, faithful and kind. Evelyn told me once that when she was five, in the early 1900s, her uncle died in rural Pennsylvania. This was before the days of embalming so funerals generally were held without much delay. The casket was open that day in the church nave just before the service and everyone said their goodbyes. But just before the benediction, Evelyn's uncle decided he'd say hello, raising himself up in the casket, alive, having been only sleeping off a long sickness that masked itself as death. Well now, I'd say that Easter was never the same for young Evelyn after that. Ditto for the uncle.

In the Book of Acts, a woman dies and comes back to life. Her name is Tabitha in Aramaic and Dorcas in Greek. Both names mean the same thing: *gazelle*. Isn't that a great name? Maybe Tabitha got her name honestly—perhaps she was fleet of foot and ran around town doing works of mercy. She apparently operated some sort of sewing cooperative that may have benefited the local town widows; in Tabitha's day, widows were generally poor, vulnerable, and on the lower rung of the economic ladder. The widows come out in great number at what they think is Tabitha's funeral, showing off her tunics and clothing as if they were at a State Fair, right there in the funeral home. Tabitha must have meant a lot to them—their beloved gazelle.

We aren't told Tabitha's age, but she reminds me of a whole generation of older women in my congregation who clearly understand the connection between discipleship and service. Tabitha, by the way, is directly named a "disciple" in verse 36 of this story, the only time in the entire New Testament that the word is rendered in the feminine. There were other female disciples of Jesus, of course, but in a man's first-century world, this citation is significant.

Another suggestive detail of the story is the setting—the seacoast town of Joppa, fifty miles northwest of Jerusalem, right on the water. Remember the Old Testament story where Joppa figures prominently? Joppa is where Jonah boards a boat in direct defiance of God's wishes. He eventually exits this boat into the sea and is swallowed and spit back out after three days and nights in the belly of a big fish. The setting of Joppa thus suggests a much older resurrection story that predates this one by several centuries.

So Tabitha dies. We aren't told how, but the community's beloved gazelle runs no more. Per the custom of the Jewish Mishnah, the widows wash her body and place her in a "room upstairs." Are we to think of that other "upper room" that was connected to the first Easter? Maybe so. Peter is summoned from a town nearby. And the widows weep openly for their friend. Tabitha had showed these women a way to live, these women whose lives seemed to be over; not just with the shirts and tunics, but with a love clearly centered in the love of Christ.

Have you ever thought much about how some deaths affect us more than others? Servicemen are killed in a helicopter crash in a town not far from mine. Scores of people die in a recent earthquake in Pakistan. Mounting evidence gathered by human rights groups suggests ethnic cleansing, genocide in Darfur. A young child is brutalized and killed by a parent. I cringe and wince when I hear about these stories. But I usually move on. We all do. Our emotions are selective or we couldn't get past the obituary page in the morning paper. The rather crass headline reports: "No Americans were injured." But this attempted fence around our national emotion is only a public revelation of what we all do privately to make it through the day. Conversely, maybe a prophet is someone who feels things so deeply and so intensely (regardless of relationship and boundary) that weeping occurs without surcease, like Jeremiah, on behalf of God and God's people. They see and feel things we don't. I am no prophet. And perhaps we should give private thanks that most of us aren't.

But who hasn't felt the deep anguish of these widows who have just lost such a close friend? I'm still getting over the death of a very close friend named Bill, about my age, who died several years ago with a brain tumor. He left a widow and two young daughters. I remember him as someone who loved the natural world, who ran everywhere he went, like a gazelle. For the longest time I found myself driving around town and suddenly breaking into tears at traffic lights. He was a companion on countless hikes and bicycle rides and conversations—a partner in prayer.

Death is all around us, and even though we are quite skilled at filtering what gets to us, some deaths penetrate our walls and shake us, even shake our faith. I prayed like anything to God, in the months before his death, that Bill, like Tabitha, would "get up" and walk with his family (and walk with me) like he once did. The image of offering his ashes to the wind, to the Spirit, in Shenandoah National Park, will never leave me.

"Tabitha, get up." And she did without a word. This turn of events is reported so matter-of-factly and simply, with no commentary. The apparent ease of biblical miracle often seems to mock the grief of our earthly existence, especially the daily reality of untimely death, unfair death. I say run quickly from any religion that promises with confident assurance: "It was their time. God needed them. They've gone to a better place." Linger instead with these widows whose eyes are worn out with weeping.

"Tabitha, get up." I find it interesting that in the New Testament the phrase "get up" is used *both* to describe a person who is beginning an act of ministry *and* a person who is raised from the dead. In this old story the text says, "Peter *got up* and went with them." It also says, "Tabitha, *get up*." Two different actions but exactly the same Greek word. According to the Bible, when we "get up" and rise for ministry in the name of Christ we are participating in a resurrection act and Easter occurs. If we follow this logic, Tabitha, Dorcas, the "gazelle," had already risen *before* she died. "She was devoted to good works and acts of charity" in Jesus' name. She did indeed rise from death—"Get up," said Peter—but in truth she had already gotten up. Jesus' love in her did it.

"Get up, Bill, please get up," I once prayed for my friend dying of cancer. It's taken me a while to say that God had actually raised Bill already, years before he died. He'd already "gotten up." Jesus' love in him did it.

Toward the very end of this story there is a final important detail. After raising "Gazelle," Peter remains in Joppa by the sea. It is fitting that Peter is now at the very westward boundary of Jewish territory. And here in this coastal town he crosses the boundary of death, but now he crosses yet another boundary. Look closely and notice where Peter now takes a room. "He stayed in Joppa for some time with a certain Simon, a tanner." And even though this seems like a rather minor detail, it isn't. Since a tanner handled the carcasses of dead animals, Simon's work was technically defiling in the eyes of an orthodox Jew. But Peter took a room there. The gospel crosses all boundaries.

o o o

One fine day in the future, after we have all breathed our last, we will hear the Lord call our names. "Get up, Bill." "Get up, Frank." "Get up, Elaine." "Get up, Elizabeth." *Get up and run like gazelles.*

It's a wonderful promise and I cannot pretend to tell you that I understand it all. But if you believe that, if you believe in that outlandish future raising beyond this world of untimely and unfair death, then maybe you'll also embrace this Bible truth:

Not only will you *be* raised, Child of God, but Christ is already *raising* you—on this side of the grave, to cross boundaries of death and bear witness to new life in a world of much sadness.

So get up. Easter not only happened once upon a time. It is happening, and our Lord is sending us to the "Joppas" of our community, the far boundaries, with a word of hope for the widows and all who think that life is over. Run like gazelles with the great good news.

For Reflection and Discussion

· *React to this claim from the essay: "The apparent ease of biblical miracle often seems to mock the grief of our earthly existence."*

· *Discuss the blessing and challenges of a selective sympathy, boundaries without which "we couldn't get past the obituary page in the morning paper."*

· *Describe how Christ may already be raising you from the dead on this side of the grave.*

> "I am the gate. Whoever enters by me will be saved, and will come in and go out and find pasture." (John 10:9)

Coming and Going

JOHN 10:1-10

Jesus says, "I am the gate." I think of the gate at the old Atlanta Stadium I used to pass through as a boy to watch Hank Aaron play—a turnstile, really, that you pushed past with a cranking sound and then you were inside a whole new country of smells and code language, signals and excitement. There was a gate that led into the backyard of my grandparents' house in Charlotte. It had a neat latch that opened up into a flower garden and my granddaddy's tool shed. A child could get lost there for hours. Once on a weeklong bicycle trip on the Blue Ridge Parkway, some friends and I came upon a gate that said the road was closed; a landslide up ahead was routing traffic all the way down through Brevard—no problem for automobiles, a daylong problem for someone on a loaded bike. We brazenly lifted our bicycles over that gate and proceeded on, an adventure that requires a bit more space and time to tell.

Of course, there are also many figurative gates we pass through. The gate that is a school bus boarded for the very first time. My wife and I have pictures of each of our three children, first day of kindergarten, climbing school bus steps, looking back to parents who were only beginning the long process of letting go. Or the gate that is marriage, the wedding day a sort of chute, a long aisle we walk down into a new life with another. Or consider the matriculation of freshmen each fall through the gates of colleges across our land, a threshold of sorts into adulthood and new responsibility. Life is largely a series of gates such as these, a chain of rather narrow choices and passageways through which we pass for better or worse.

Jesus says, "I am the gate." And maybe his use of a definite article suggests that this little word "the" should actually be capitalized: THE gate. For many Christians, of course, such a claim is more threat than promise. You're either in or you're out—on one side of the gate or (alas) the other. Jesus is the Great Gatekeeper in the Sky, the Heavenly Divider, who will one day count heads and woe to those on the *wrong* side. And so let go of that pew, sinner man, and come through the gate that is Jesus before it's too late.

I really have no problem with Jesus as Judge. It says right in the creed that he'll do this. My problem is that he keeps siding with people I don't like a whole lot, people clearly outside the sheepfold it seems to me, and to tell you the truth, this infuriates me. I was eating breakfast in a Hardee's restaurant several years back, innocently munching on a sausage biscuit, sipping coffee, and reading the newspaper, when I came across a little article far from the headlines that reported the baptism of Jeffrey Dahmer in a prison in Portage, Wisconsin. The nautical imagery from the town name did not soften the outrage of such a baptism. You remember Dahmer. If anyone's on the other side of the gate, here's our man. And yet his eleventh-hour confession washes everything away? If that's the case, then Jesus the Gate is a rather torn and rickety screen door that lets a lot of flies in.

"I am the gate," says Jesus. "Whoever enters by me will be saved." Ah, and there's the very word: *saved*. It's appealing to read these

verses and play the old game of who's in and who's out. Who's safely
on the right side of the gate, in the pasture of Jesus' bosom, and who's
not. "Brother, are you saved? Sister, are you right with Jesus?" So
much of what passes for Christianity centers upon saving souls for
another life. "In or out? Choose now," we're often told. "Your eternity
hangs in the balance."

But there is a little phrase in this verse that should forever dis-
rupt the sure certainties of anyone who only sees eternity here. "I am
the gate." Got it. "Whoever enters by me will be saved." No problem
there. But here comes the line: such people "will come in and go out
and find pasture."

Come in *and* go out? Now wait a minute. Jesus is a gate and you
come in and you huddle together with other like-minded believers
and you wait to be whisked away to heaven, right? Whatever do you
mean, "go out"? My Bible says that Jesus is the Gate, not some sort of
revolving door for Pete's sake.

And see, it's those two little words that really ought to scram-
ble our whole perception of what Christianity, church, and salvation (all three) are really all about. Those who enter through the
gate that is Jesus will come in *and* go out and find pasture. So with
Jesus you'll find pasture whether you're coming or going. With Jesus
you'll find pasture in the safe confines of the sheepfold, the congregation, with the wonderful *alma mater* hymns, but also out in the
world of your Monday and Tuesday. With Jesus it's all pasture potentially. With Jesus there's not a nook or cranny of your week where the
man isn't.

To be honest, this may not be good news. This is a terrifying and
terrifically burdensome idea for some. Sunday morning is just about
all the church many of us can stand. You might remember old Peter,
out fishing on his day job, minding his own business before Jesus
shows up and teaches him a new way to cast. After striking out all
night, the flounder are now flopping all over the bottom of the boat.
And do you remember Peter's reaction? Is he happy about this? No,
he's not. He's scared out of his wits. "Go away from me, Lord," he
says. "I'm a sinful man" (Luke 5:8). Peter realizes that God cannot be

compartmentalized into a little Sabbath slot any longer. There's just not a place where Jesus isn't. Good news? Well, maybe.

"I am the gate. Whoever enters by me will be saved and will come in *and* go out and find pasture." One of the reasons that many churches are so diminished here early in the twenty-first century is that our perception of Jesus and his claim upon our lives is often so stunted. Our definitions betray us. "Church" becomes an hour-long worship service and "salvation" is some shadowy future realm where God counts heads. Is it any wonder that such a limited perception of Christian community fails to attract many converts? Until churches make the vital crossover into *everything* that encompasses our "going out" (as well as our "coming in"), we will continue to scratch our heads and wonder why people aren't lining up at the gate—the gate that is Jesus.

The New Testament describes our Lord in this fashion: "When he was abused, he did not return abuse; when he suffered, he did not threaten" (1 Peter 2:23). Jesus lived in this world in a distinct and peculiar way. His life was not a walk in the park, but even as he suffered, he was able to find pasture—to forgive even as others were killing him. "Follow me," he says. How do we help people live out the practical implications of following Jesus "out there" in the daily give and take of life? Life where we are sometimes used wrongly by others, a life where we sometimes suffer? Answering such a question is a primary purpose of any congregation as Christians huddle together "in here." We come through the gate that is Jesus, and our perspective on everything changes, not just the obviously holy hours of life—all of it. Coming and going we find pasture.

Several years ago I went to see a play about the life of Dietrich Bonhoeffer. We recently celebrated the 60th anniversary of his death. If you know the man, you'll recall that he left his rather safe studies in New York City in the late 1930s to work for the resistance movement that defied Hitler. Why in the world did he do that? Well, it had something to with Jesus. Bonhoeffer knew what was at stake and could not remain silent, but when he returned to his native Germany, he soon discovered a rather surprising challenge from an unforeseen source: the church. This is the line from the play that really shook me. "It's not Hitler who needs to be converted to Jesus!" Bonhoeffer thundered. "It's *Christians* who need conversion."

Bonhoeffer's plea to the churches is still a modern challenge: to come through the gate that is Christ will now affect everything—*everything* we do and see. Here, now. If Jesus is the gate that swings in and out, we cannot conveniently place him on a Sunday shelf or catalog him, as in a dictionary, under the word "heaven." Frederick Buechner writes: "You do not love God and live for him so you will go to Heaven. Whichever side of the grave you happen to be talking about, to love God and live for him *is* heaven."[46]

"I am the gate," says Jesus. "Whoever enters by me will be saved, and will come in and go out and find pasture."

Coming or going, it's all about Jesus, our gate to abundant life.

For Reflection and Discussion

- *What sort of feelings surface when you hear the theological word "saved"?*

- *React to the Frederick Buechner quote near the end of this essay.*

- *If God is our ultimate judge, why do you think so many Christians tend to "count heads" concerning who may be in or out of heaven?*

TIME AFTER PENTECOST

Time after Pentecost

In his marvelous book *Finally Comes the Poet*, Walter Brueggemann reflects upon the character and faith of Daniel and the political setting of the book that bears his name. The children of God are in exile, miles from home in Babylon. This presents a crisis for the religious community, and the writing reveals the theological mettle of people under fire for their faith.

The community experiences foreign threats, fiery furnaces, and dens of lions. How do they survive such assaults on their faith? "Individual persons," writes Brueggemann, "are able to withstand the pressure of persecution and its depersonalization because they have an identity that is beyond the reach of the persecutor . . . persons of faith need not believe or accept the identity that their persecutors want to give them."[47]

Pentecost, the gift of the Holy Spirit to once-timid disciples (Acts 2:1-21), and the Time after Pentecost is the longest season of the church year—"ordinary time" in which the church experiences growth in commitment and discipleship. This growth often occurs without notice, much like the farmer who experiences that "The earth produces of itself" (Mark 4:28; the Greek word is *automate*) in mystery and wonder. Something happened to Peter at the first Pentecost that caused a shy, nervous man full of denial to speak up for Jesus in the same streets (before the same threat of persecution!) just a few weeks later.

Every hymn we sing, every prayer we pray, every Eucharist we celebrate, and every Bible story we read contribute to shaping our Christian identity that at some point matures "beyond the reach of the persecutor." A church whose identity is intact is convinced that nothing can truly "get" us—not untimely illness or some shadowy future death or the darkness of sinister terrorism. This is a wonderfully liberating realization. The Time after Pentecost frees us to sing and loosens our tongues to give testimony to another reality, another kingdom where God reigns above all earthly powers.

HE WAS TRYING TO SEE WHO JESUS WAS . . . SO HE RAN AHEAD
AND CLIMBED A SYCAMORE TREE. (LUKE 19:3-4)

The Church as Tree House

LUKE 19:1-10

ON A RECENT THURSDAY morning I traveled just up the road to our local Lutheran seminary and heard a remarkable lecture offered by the Center on Religion in the South. The lecture was titled, "Civic Virtue: The Role of Religion in Brown Versus Board of Education."

Americans celebrated the 50th anniversary of that famous Kansas court case in 2004, a landmark case that led to public school desegregation across the country. What I had forgotten, or maybe never knew, is that the roots of that decision in Topeka began in my home state of South Carolina, just down the road in Clarendon County.

The sons of Pastor Joseph Delaine spoke movingly about their father, who served a congregation near Summerton, South Carolina, and was principal of the all-black school just north of town. Reverend Delaine had the gospel audacity to suggest that all children have equal access to quality public education. And he refused to keep quiet about that conviction. The sons recalled the numerous threats to their dad's life. They recalled the many instances of vandalism at their home, the church parsonage. They recalled in sadness the day the church building, the place where they worshipped and went to Sunday School, was burned to the ground by local arsonists furious with their father. Fifty years later, it's still fair to ask: *How do people change?*

Having lived for almost twenty years in Virginia, I knew of the town of Farmville, a notoriously segregated area of the state well after the events of the civil rights movement. Two weeks before the seminary lecture, I heard a remarkable interview on National Public Radio about that very community. Juan Williams was interviewing an older matriarch of a prominent Farmville family, a family that had defended white supremacy and southern tradition for generations in their corner of the world. Up until very recently, it was not safe to go into Farmville after dark if you were black. But in the radio interview, this woman recalled the rage and anger of her now deceased husband as she bounced her newly adopted grandchild on her lap—a little biracial boy whose African American blood would surely have made his grandfather's boil. But here he was, grafted into this family. And so I ask again, in wonder: *How do people change?*

One of the most popular Bible stories of all time stars the diminutive favorite of Christian kindergartners everywhere, that wee man who climbed a sycamore tree to get a better view of Jesus.[48] You might want to be careful with this story, however. Just as we tend to sugar-coat Noah and his famous ark, remembering only rainbows and forgetting the flood, it's easy to overlook the unsavory details of the story, how truly despicable and despised Zacchaeus actually was. The little man was a *"chief* tax collector," the only time in the New Testament such an adjective is used to describe an already unpopular occupation. Zacchaeus apparently was the head-honcho cheat, the consummate crook, vilified and hated by most everyone in town. I always think of the actor Danny DeVito when reading this gospel tale.

But I also think of that part of my own life that resists change and engages in unsavory behavior. These old stories are meant to mirror our own, so it's always important to locate our own lives therein. Teenagers of your acquaintance will understand this rather weak connection to the "Austin Powers" movies. In finding your place in this old story, you might think of Zacchaeus as a "Mini-Me" of sorts, a replica of our own reprobation. That's you shimmying up the sycamore with all your bad habits; that's me with mine. So let's ask the question once more on our way up: *How do people change?*

Now don't forget the setting of this old story. Jesus is passing through Jericho. Remember what happened there a millennium or so prior to the scaling of this sycamore? The walls of Jericho tumbled down when Joshua blew his mighty horn. Other walls are about to crumble as the new Joshua strides through town. (Jericho, by the way, is less than twenty miles from Jerusalem as the crow flies. And the following Friday, less than a week after Zacchaeus climbs this sycamore, Jesus will climb his own tree—the tree that is his cross. Many walls are starting to crumble there in Jericho.)

So Zacchaeus is out on the branch, we're out on the branch, waiting for Jesus to pass by. But back up just a bit. Just before the climb, the story includes a single little word (a single syllable) that sheds all sorts of light on the question I keep asking. In verse 3 we're told that because of his stature the little man was trying like anything, jumping up and down perhaps, even poking his shrewd little head into the spaces between taller people's legs, in order to "see who Jesus *was*." It never says that he was just trying to see the man, the way you'd try to get a quick glimpse of one of the Red Sox in a rare World Series parade. Zacchaeus was apparently after more than that. He was trying to see *who Jesus was*. What he was truly about. He was not after his autograph, in other words. He wanted more than a peek at a great man. Zacchaeus wanted something more.

It strikes me that this was exactly the spiritual posture of a restless Martin Luther early in his career. He wanted to see for himself *who Jesus was*. He wasn't content with glimpses, occasional peeks, or second-hand reports. He needed to know for himself, first-hand. Luther knew early on what Zacchaeus knew and what all authentic sinners know. Jesus will do the work in us, will change and transform us, but we must want that, at least a little bit.

Jesus is not a magician. He cannot wiggle his nose and say *Poof*, new Zacchaeus, new Martin Luther, or new Frank. *Brown v. the Topeka Board of Education* did not happen overnight. No reformation ever has. We must be willing to place ourselves in situations and circumstances so that we can truly see *who Jesus is*.

"Zacchaeus, hurry and come down; for I must stay at your house today." Jesus enters the homes of crooks and eats with them. It's not a bad description of the Eucharist. Jesus enters a house, the church, and eats with us; the house with a tree at the very center. One can argue that unless we encounter Jesus from the branches of the tree that is the cross, we will never truly see who Jesus is. We might get a peek here and there, but without the cross in our lives it's always like watching some famous figure in a distant convertible, waving to us with the placard "Son of God" taped to the door as the parade files by, observed from a safe and comfortable distance.

How *do* people change? How do we go about forming Zaccheuses, Zaccheii, who live life differently? After his encounter with Jesus, the generosity of Zacchaeus is astounding. He parts with his wealth and begins to live for others.

Jesus can remodel the house that is the church. "I'm coming to your house today," Jesus says. We need only let him in—into every room, every space—until the branches of his healing tree flower and embrace us all.

For Reflection and Discussion

- *Try to describe any changes that may be occurring in you as a result of your new affiliation with Jesus.*

- *Look closely in this story at the radical generosity of Zacchaeus. What general principles about sharing and financial security can you draw from these verses?*

- *What is the difference between "looking at" Jesus and attempting to "see who Jesus is"?*

BUT HE WAS IN THE STERN, ASLEEP ON THE CUSHION; AND THEY WOKE HIM UP AND SAID TO HIM, "TEACHER, DO YOU NOT CARE THAT WE ARE PERISHING?" (MARK 4:38)

2

Storm Snoring

MARK 4:35-41

THERE HE WAS, SOUND asleep on a little pillow. Waves crashing over the bow of the little boat, wind blowing overboard anything not tied down, grown men hollering and hanging on for dear life, cursing under their breath, water pooling at their feet. And Jesus sleeps like a baby through it all. "Is there anything else we can get for you, Jesus? Are you comfy? Cozy? All tucked in over there? Should we break out a Sealy Posturepedic mattress for you? How about a blanket or a smoking jacket? Maybe a glass of sherry? Wouldn't want you to be disturbed here in any way."

It doesn't take a rocket scientist to detect the mocking and derisive tones of these fearful disciples. They are about to meet their maker and their leader snoozes right through wind and wave, his head on a little cushion. Please pay close attention to this contrast between all these chickens with their heads cut off, racing around filled with complete terror, and our Lord who seems able to sleep through just about anything.

I'm reminded of a youth backpacking trip I led several years ago where two of the teenagers carried one of these new freestanding tents that do not require tent stakes. Sometime during the night they rolled over in such a way that when we woke up the next morning, the tent was completely inverted, and they were sleeping on the roof. It was quite a sight. I guess some people can sleep through anything. Maybe Jesus fits this category.

Anyway, these justifiably fearful men can't stand it anymore and wake their leader up. "Teacher, do you not care that we are perishing?" For my money, that is one of the most loaded questions in the human language. *Don't you care about us?* There are few words that carry more emotional baggage than the word "care." We church folk strive to be perceived as people who care. We care about world hunger. We care about sick people on our prayer list. We care about the state of the environment. We at least wince, don't we? Never let it be said that church people are uncaring. We're in the business of caring. That's what the church is for, isn't it? That we should care for others and maybe receive some of that care ourselves in a crisis? It's hard to imagine someone who loves Jesus reacting with indifference. There are few charges that confront our faith more than this one: *You don't care about me.* Soap operas tap into this well: "You don't care about me, do you John? In fact, you've never cared about me. That's so obvious to me now. You only care about *her.*"

"Don't you care about us, Jesus? We're about to die here. Think you might rub the sleep out of your eyes long enough to help us?" Jesus cared about people. You don't have to read very far in the Bible to discover that. But here in the boat he seems completely unconcerned, completely at peace, while the disciples struggle with a storm that is about to kill them. Why does he do this? Why isn't Jesus protecting them, shielding them, warding off every danger and calamity?

It doesn't take a theological prodigy to begin asking the same questions about our own lives. We're believers, right? Why doesn't

Jesus protect us from cancer, from pain, from evil, from any number of storms that blow into our lives? Is he asleep or something? Was Thomas Jefferson (the famous deist) right when he suggested that God wound up the world like a clockmaker but really doesn't participate in daily details? *Don't you care, Jesus?* Then why is this happening? The question asked from the center of that storm is also our own. The questions, indeed, are as old as Job. The Greek word for "windstorm" in this story is the very same word as "whirlwind" from the Greek Old Testament (Septuagint) version in Job 38:1. The disciples are questioning Jesus in a fashion similar to the way that Job once questioned God.

One of my favorite poets is a man named Andrew Hudgins who teaches at Ohio State. Lately I've been reading his autobiography where he recalls from his childhood a great love for the "Hardy Boys" mystery series. "I can still summon," writes Hudgins, "the dismay I felt when I discovered that F. W. Dixon was not really the author of the Hardy Boys books but a pseudonym for many different writers working to a formula. I felt that some tacit agreement had been violated, some faith betrayed. I'd trusted F. W. Dixon, merged my nervous system with his sentences and stories until I was oblivious to the world outside them, and then I found out he didn't exist. O, cruel and faithless F. W. Dixon!"[49]

I'm convinced that something like this often happens with Christian believers who discover that Jesus isn't the person we thought he was. We read about the man who walks on water, feeds five thousand, and raises little girls from the dead. The Jesus we experience from day to day doesn't seem to be the same character we experience in the pages of scripture. I don't care how strong your faith may be—we've all wondered why Jesus doesn't just swoop down and fix things, especially for churchgoing people like us. Shouldn't we be granted some special exemption from suffering since we are followers of Jesus?

As you know, Jesus does finally wake up in this story. He quiets wind and wave. It's a miracle, all is well, the disciples get what they wanted, and you'd think the story could end right there. But it doesn't. There may be calm on the water, but not in the boat. Anytime you see the word "boat" in the gospels, also think "church." Many church buildings were designed to look like an inverted boat. With that in mind: the water may be calm, but the tension in the boat is so thick that you can cut it with a knife.

"Why are you afraid? Have you still no faith?" It's curious. Jesus doesn't say a word about the storm, doesn't mention the water pooled at their feet, doesn't even bother to acknowledge that they almost lost their lives out there; the philosophical ponderings about suffering are not even on his radar screen. Jesus wants to know about their faith.

"Miracle" is a word that is far too narrowly defined, reserved for paranormal interruptions in the natural order. This story hardly highlights the stilling of wind and wave, the very things these fearful disciples wanted most. What they desired is what we usually want from Jesus: an immediate release from our predicament.

But there is a greater miracle afoot here, only foreshadowed in the story. Jesus is concerned with the faith resources his followers will use in the midst of the storm *even more than the storm itself.* Jesus seems to be asking his disciples, "When trouble comes your way, how will you manage? How will you deal with fear and anxiety and frustration when they come along?" And these things will come to all of us, sooner or later. These questions seem to be Jesus' concerns throughout the gospels. His miracles are not the main thing. The real miracle is the mature faith formed in his disciples, faith that is able to withstand any storm. A church worth its salt is less about waiting for Jesus to pull off another miracle and more about forming disciples who are equipped with a faith mature enough to weather storms.

Jesus slept well in the middle of a storm not because he was tired, but because he was confident—confident in the abiding care of God.

Blessed are those at sea who have such a faith.

No matter what happens to them, they will sleep well.

For Reflection and Discussion

- *The seeming absence of Jesus in the storms of life is a huge theological question. Why doesn't Jesus just swoop down and fix things?*

- *Elaborate on this sentence from the essay: "Jesus is concerned with the faith resources his followers will use in the midst of the storm even more than the storm itself."*

- *If Christianity cannot provide a special exemption from suffering, and if faith is not an inoculation from evil, why do you bother with Jesus?*

3

Pledging Allegiance

LUKE 9:51-62

OKAY, BE HONEST. IS there anything that Jesus ever said that seems more rude, more unfeeling and harsh than these words? I'd be glad to accept other nominations for that award, but this story has my vote. Let's see if I've got this straight. Jesus is heading towards Jerusalem; he "set his face" towards the city and you know what happens there. These admonitions are from a block of teaching known as the "Travel Narrative" in the gospel of Luke. Jesus is on the road from chapter 9 of this gospel through chapter 19, and we're invited to walk along with him and learn what it means to be a disciple.

Jesus begins this journey and right off the bat encounters three would-be disciples—possible converts, potential church members we might call them. One says, "Lord, I'd be glad to hit the road with you, but I've got to bury my dad first." It's a reasonable request, isn't it? Is this man not partially fulfilling the fourth Commandment, honoring Mom and Dad? "I'm coming," says this man. "I'll be there, but first let me take care of this one little thing." Request denied.

Now come on; the funeral couldn't have taken that long. And then comes the zinger. "Let the dead bury their own dead." Now what is that? Can you imagine saying that out loud to someone you know who is grieving the death of a loved one? These words seem so un-Jesus-like. I was in a Bible study once, and we were discussing this passage. No one could ever quite understand our Lord's apparent lack of compassion. In jest, one member of the group said he believed "Jesus should be soundly spanked and sent to bed."

Maybe Jesus was just having a bad day. Maybe it was hot out there on the road to Jerusalem, and he had a headache. Maybe he did what we all do when we have a snappy retort lodged in our minds, a pithy comeback that we're thinking but would never say out loud—only this time it slipped for Jesus, and he came right out with it.

I read this passage and I begin to rationalize. I begin to make excuses for Jesus and tell myself that this is surely some anomaly. Surely a unique episode, out of place, and Jesus is just having a bad hair day. So I forage around in the New Testament a bit, hoping to find nothing, and I discover that this is no anomaly at all. In fact, it's a running theme! Over and again in the gospels, Jesus confronts the coziness and limits of family.

Case #1—In Matthew, Jesus says, "You thought I came to bring peace? Think again. I came to set sons against fathers, daughters against mothers ..."[50] and so on. Why does Jesus seem intent on splitting up the family?

Case #2—Mark reports early in his gospel that Jesus' family is wondering whether he has gone off the deep end, a little nuts. Mary and the siblings come looking for him. A message is relayed: "Your mother and brothers are outside." Jesus' answer is a rather shocking slap in the face to his family and maybe any family. "Who are my mother and my brothers?" he asks. Looking around at those who sat near him, he says, "Here are my mother and my brothers! Whoever does the will of God is my brother and sister and mother."[51]

Case #3—I noticed on a recent Labor Day Weekend (when families were enjoying the last hurrah of summer together) that the gospel reading from Luke that Sunday happened to be these jarring words: "Whoever comes to me and does not *hate* father and mother, wife and children, etc., cannot be my disciple." [52] Oh my.

I could cite other passages, but these are enough to say the following with some rather clear conviction—Jesus did not utter this particular teaching about a funeral protocol because he was having a bad day. This is no bolt out of the blue. It seems to a running biblical *pattern*. It always amuses me in public elections when Jesus' name is invoked as the preeminent upholder of "family values." I'm not so sure he would interview all that well on one of those Dr. Dobson "Focus on the Family" radio talk shows. For some reason our Lord was undeniably tough on the nuclear family. The question we must ask so many centuries later is why.

I love my mom and dad. We just celebrated their 50th anniversary (no small accomplishment these days) and told all the old stories that cement us together as a family. I love my family, my wife and children. There is perhaps no more instinctual love for any of us. But here's the thing. And this is what Jesus is getting at, I think.

If I love my family—my mother and father, my wife and children—*more* than Christ and allow that familial love (no matter how pure or well-intentioned) to supersede my following of Jesus, then you know what? I will ultimately be unable to do my family much good. *Some good*, yes. But unless I place Christ first and learn from him how to love others, including my own family, then my attempts at love will always be too limiting, maybe too suffocating, even blinding me to the needs of others who are also my "family" according to our theology of baptism. Jesus was downright passionate about this sort of family: the family of God. In this family kinfolk don't just live "over the river and through the woods" but all the way to Baghdad, all the way to El Salvador, all the way to the West Bank, all the way to Somalia. This family of God is much bigger and much older than the way we usually define a family. It is built not by birth but by baptism.

Whenever a person "joins the church," it is to this new family that a person pledges primary allegiance. Not because we are to ignore those blood kin living under our respective roofs, but because we cannot give them the love they need until Jesus and his kingdom are first. We just can't pull it off alone. Without Jesus at the center, we can frankly smother one another in lavish excess in the name of "love."

Jesus sets his face towards Jerusalem. In the gospel of Luke, we hear strong words from Jesus about what it means to be a disciple. You notice I didn't say "church member." I said *disciple*. To be a church member in the American context is frankly often about as threatening as Melba Toast. We are in trouble today all across the church because we have confused discipleship with membership. Membership suggests occasional affiliation, and that's about it. Discipleship demands our primary allegiance.

I realize that Jesus sounds harsh at times. The following requests sound exceedingly reasonable. "But first let me bury my father." "First let me say farewell to those at home." With rather abrupt language, Jesus is pressing us here to examine what's truly first. For Christians, authentic disciples, it is the family of God that must take first priority. Perhaps our American families are in such a mess today because we have forgotten this, allowing so many other things, false idols, to take priority in our lives.

Hear this: one of the least obvious but most pervasive idols in this country is the god of family. We often place the family's security and comfort first before anything else—and we ironically run low on the one thing that can truly save us all: the love and teachings of Christ.

Jesus wants us to love our families. But a family simply cannot love each other adequately just by themselves. We will always need a much bigger family, a much larger landscape in which to love and learn.

The Bible calls this the family of God, the wide kingdom of our risen Lord.

For Reflection and Discussion

- *How is it possible for family members to smother one another in the name of love?*

- *"One of the least obvious but most pervasive idols in this country is the god of family." Do you agree or disagree with this statement? Why?*

- *In much popular Christian art, Jesus always seems like such a sweet, smiling man. Why might we sometimes need a rude Jesus?*

"SO I SAY TO YOU, ASK, AND IT WILL BE GIVEN YOU; SEARCH, AND YOU WILL FIND; KNOCK, AND THE DOOR WILL BE OPENED FOR YOU." (LUKE 11:9)

Keeping At It

4

LUKE 11:1-13

ASK. SEARCH. KNOCK. ARE these old words of Jesus really true? I've known people who tell me they've asked God for many things for many years, receiving only silence. I've known people who say they've engaged in serious theological searches with no clear discoveries. I've known people who report they have knocked and knocked quite patiently and could not open any door.

I have an old article from *The Washington Post* that I keep handy in a file. It was written by a man who had a very sick baby in intensive care. He wanted to help his child, but this young father had a hard time praying. He wrote: "Family in Maine prays, friends in Oregon pray, whole congregations say 'Lord, hear our prayer' when the priest announces Alex's name and condition. My wife's sister, a master of theological studies candidate, has mobilized the whole faculty and student body to petition God on my son's behalf. Certainly I should join in. It seems reasonable, expected. That's the wonderful thing about prayer: It's easy to sneak one in—just think it. I look at Alex again. His [situation] seems tailor-made to pull a prayer from a tired father's soul. Only a monster would fail. I lean against the wall again and look out the window. I cannot do it."[53]

Why do you suppose this young father could not pray for his critically ill son? Perhaps he is agnostic about God and/or prayer, even in this particular foxhole. Why do you suppose many people intend to pray, would even agree out loud that prayer is important, but never really get around to it? An avalanche of the mundane takes practical priority over prayer in a given week. We mean to pray, even want to pray more, but usually don't. Perhaps our lack of attention to prayer reveals what no one is willing to say out loud. And a final question. Why, come to think of it, pray at all if God knows our needs even before we voice them?

Here's an idea I've been thinking about a lot lately that may get at the heart of each question. Ponder this idea with me. More than any other single action, *how we pray reveals most clearly our true beliefs about God and what we really think God is capable of doing in this world.* Now what do I mean by that?

Well, just this. It's possible for a person to fake worship. Mumble the creed and you're home soon enough. A person can even fake church membership. Commune a couple times per year and make a single contribution of record, and we'll keep you on the rolls in the Lutheran tradition. Our constitution says so. I can even fake a sermon. Online homilies abound if I were so inclined. Probably no one would ever know. My point is that a lot of what passes for modern Christianity can be faked (or endured) without thinking about it too much.

One thing a person cannot fake, however, is prayer. No one is there to check up on you. You either do it, or you don't. When it's just me and God alone in my private place, the words and hopes I share with God (or the lack of them) reveal more about my real convictions concerning how God works in the world than a host of Sunday mornings ever could.

Prayer is the place where we are most truly ourselves with God. No one is there to check up on the theological orthodoxy of your prayer. No one is waiting to say, "No, you can't pray that." If you really want to find an accurate gauge that will measure one's true and honest beliefs abut the divine, examine closely the content of your prayers. It's possible to fake a lot in church life, but you can't fake prayer. How we pray reveals what we truly believe about God.

In this lesson from Luke we are given some rather peculiar advice about prayer. Jesus advises his disciples to be persistent like the friend who will not go away until he gets his neighbor out of bed at midnight to borrow a few groceries. I say that any guest who arrives that late can wait for breakfast, but the idea seems to be that our prayers are at least somewhat important in getting God to take action. God is good, says Jesus. Ask him yourself for what you need. Even evil parents give good things to their kids. Look how much more you can expect from God. "So ask, search, knock," says Jesus. "Tell God what's on your mind."

Maybe you're wondering why you need to ask God for these things in the first place. Can I really rouse God to action and change God's mind like Abraham once did at Sodom (Genesis 18:22-33) if I just badger the dickens out of the Lord? Abraham talks God down six times in this old narrative (I counted). Several of these six times finds Abraham reminding God of God's own job description! Talk about uppity prayer. "Far be it from you to do such a thing," Abraham says. "Far be that from you! Shall not the Judge of the whole earth do what is just?" I can picture someone like Woody Allen loving this scene. Abraham appears to be talking to a wayward child, not the author of the entire cosmos. And Abraham survives the encounter!

So, yes, I think we're given a green light in these stories to take it all before God. Lay it right out with unedited honesty. Please quit praying with your best manners. God knows you don't sound that way in your normal voice. But a question remains.

Does God wait until we pray for something before acting? Do we really need to badger God or does God already know our needs and hopes before bringing them to voice? Why bother to pray, for example, for people on a congregational prayer list? Why doesn't God just go ahead and heal them? Why do we have to ask and knock in the first place?

Apparently God *likes* us to ask. For prayer to matter, we must really want what we are praying for. That may sound silly, and we admittedly do not always get what we want in prayer even when we ask with honesty, search until we drop, and knock until our knuckles are bloody. David James Duncan writes: "As for the time I asked Jesus for a base hit at a ball game, when I stepped to the plate and struck out on three pitches I was relieved: if every kid in America could get a hit just by asking Jesus, we'd all bat a thousand and ruin baseball in a day."[54] But God, evidently, likes for us to ask. God needs to know if we really want what we're praying for.

Let me give you an example of what I'm saying. Look at three little words from that famous prayer Jesus shares with his disciples: "Your kingdom come." We usually pray these words with such ease. But do we actually realize what we're asking for here? *Your kingdom come.* What would it mean if God's kingdom really did come in all its fullness? What would have to change in the world as we now know it? What would be redistributed? How would our own lives look different? Do we really *want* the kingdom to come right now? Do we really want the outsider to be included, do we want the wealth of this world to be redistributed, do we want the last to be first and the discarded to become family? (If not, maybe we should stop praying that prayer.)

And see, that's what I'm talking about. God likes for us to ask, search, and knock because God needs to know. For prayer to matter we must really want what we're praying for. So before a couple *asks* God for healing in their marriage, they need to be utterly honest about whether they truly want healing. Before a congregation *searches* for a new direction in its ministry, those collected disciples must be honest about whether they will truly invest the time and energy required to make changes, or whether they want change at all. Before *knocking* angrily on the many doors of injustice and poverty in the world, an individual must take stock of whether there's an honest will to make a shift in personal lifestyle that spends far too much on the self.

God is not a magician. In some early frescoes depicting the raising of Lazarus, Jesus actually stands outside the grave with a little wand.[55] But no, God is not a magician. For prayer to matter (and that's different, by the way, from being "successful"), we must really want what we're praying for.

So ask, search, and knock—all three. Someone once said: "Prayer is trying to tell the truth."

We should never be more honest than we are in prayer.

For Reflection and Discussion

- *Try to define the word "prayer."*

- *Reflect upon this question from the essay: "Why pray at all if God knows our needs even before we voice them?"*

- *Why is it difficult (if not impossible) to "fake" prayer?*

ELIJAH GOT UP, AND ATE AND DRANK; THEN HE WENT IN THE STRENGTH OF THAT FOOD FORTY DAYS AND FORTY NIGHTS.
(1 KINGS 19:8)

5

Non-Perishable Food

1 KINGS 19:1-14

THERE IS A VARIETY OF clinical explanations for those who suffer from chronic depression. Born into a family whose genetic makeup is a virtual time-bomb waiting to go off in generational fits and starts, I'm fairly well acquainted with the vast body of literature on the subject. We have learned more about depression and the intricate circuitry of the human brain in the last thirty years than in the last thirty centuries combined. Our national vocabulary now includes strange-sounding words such as "serotonin" and "neurotransmitter." We have access to a cornucopia of drugs with names that read like planets encountered by the crew of the starship *Enterprise*—names like Prozac and Paxil and Zoloft. In short, we know more about what Winston Churchill once called "The Black Dog" than ever before. It's unclear whether St. John's Wort actually works. But it's fairly certain that these days we won't mistake this herbal supplement for a dermatological relic once removed from the nose or big toe of the writer of the Fourth Gospel, who may have handled one too many toads (you may have to think about that one a moment).

With some mild reservation guarding obvious abuse, I generally say praise God for this information and these strides in pharmacological discovery. Soon after the death of her father, my mother was prowling through the attic of her childhood home in North Carolina and came across evidence of an aunt (my grandfather's sister) who my mother never knew existed. Aunt Eulie was admitted to a sanitarium near Memphis in the 1920s, and no one spoke about her within earshot of the children ever again. By the time my mother tracked her down, Eulie was an old woman, unable to speak or communicate. This is not an unusual story. Mental illness is still only whispered about in many families. Blessedly, we have made great strides in bringing depression (and its related cousins) out of the closet and embracing those who suffer from it in the church.

I find it interesting that Elijah the prophet, hiding out in a cave, seems to be a man who exhibits all the signs of clinical depression— isolation, despair, even thoughts of suicide. His prayer seems hopeless: "It is enough; now, O Lord, take away my life." Elijah is certainly not alone in the Bible among those who suffered with this affliction. Many of the Psalms, for example, are filled with utter despair. Job's trials and tribulations cause him to spiral into profound darkness and the very brink of a complete loss of faith. The writer of Ecclesiastes writes as honestly and poignantly about meaninglessness as anyone in either testament. And some suspect that St. Paul's ambiguous "thorn in the flesh" (about which he prayed many times) may be a veiled reference to his own struggles with depression.

Sometimes it's difficult to pinpoint exactly why people become depressed, but in Elijah's case the Bible offers several specific hints. What led Elijah into the wilderness, to this "solitary broom tree," to the very depths of despondency? In the eighteenth chapter of First Kings, we learn that the Israelites were once again waffling in their allegiance to God and running after another deity. So Elijah proposes an elaborate contest, a divine standoff on the summit of a nearby mountain. He tells 450 prophets of Baal to stack wood in a pile. Elijah then gathers his own stack; but to underscore the folly of taking on God, the prophet orders a drenching of his wood not once, not twice, but three times until the water drips off the timber and fills the trench surrounding the altar to the brim. Who will successfully detonate the wood with fire? Baal or Yahweh?

The prophets of Baal go first. After multiple prayer gyrations, including body piercings and bloodlettings, and not even a spark from the heavens, Elijah offers a series of taunts. "Hey guys, maybe your god is asleep or something. Maybe he's been delayed. Maybe he's in the bathroom."[56] It's all right there in the Bible. Now it's Elijah's turn. He calls on the name of the Lord. "Nothing was left of the offering," says one commentator, "but a pile of ashes and a smell like the Fourth of July."[57] Queen Jezebel, a notorious bad girl of the Bible (don't you love her name?), is furious with Elijah for showing up her boys and vows to have our hero's head within 24 hours. The prophet flees into the wilderness and gives up—exhausted, worn out, ready to end his life.

There are a variety of reasons that explain the origins of depression including genetics, chemical imbalance, or unexpected and painful crisis—loss of job, loss of family member, loss of faith. But Elijah's story reveals another reason. Elijah's depression has its roots in his own faithfulness. He is brought to the brink of giving up not because of what he did wrong, but because of *what he did right*. Elijah can only focus on his perceived worthlessness. God, however, has other plans for the prophet.

It's hard to hear the truth about ourselves. But it's even harder to tell others the truth. Depression may raise its ugly head for a variety of reasons, but sometimes it's because we've tried to tell the truth (in the family, in the workplace, in the church) and people just don't want to hear it. Elijah was depressed not for what he did wrong, but for what he did right. He was pretty convinced that he was alone in standing up for God. "I've been very zealous for you God," he says a bit later in the story. "I alone am left."

Sometimes life as a disciple leads down Elijah's path. You make an unpopular stand in speaking up for justice, and no one seems to care or really listen. You have a passion for Jesus, a zeal for real depth of discipleship, and others go the other way when they see you coming, content to play it safe in church year after year. You come up with a great idea for ministry, a wonderful new direction for the congregation, and it just gets lost in layer upon layer of debate and endless decision-making until you give up and wonder if there's any use.

Depression rears its dark head for many reasons. "Just have faith," you sometimes hear, "and God will solve all your problems." But I sometimes wonder if an overlooked reason for depression is not so much faith*less*ness as faith*ful*ness—the reality of living as a person of faith in a world like ours that typically crucifies its prophets. Perhaps occasional depression is a normal by-product of a life that truly takes Jesus seriously—the sometimes depressing theological disconnect between the biblical teachings of Jesus and the entrenched priorities of God's people who've been seduced by the world. When it comes right down to it, we undeniably live in a culture that invokes a variety of other gods to light our fires. The priests of Baal still beckon.

But watch closely how God responds to Elijah's depression brought on by faithfulness. Watch the angel. Notice that the angel keeps coming back—once and then a second time—to remind Elijah who he is. Notice that the angel doesn't try to "fix" everything or play amateur therapist or assure Elijah that this won't happen again. Notice that the angel will not allow Elijah to give in, but instead gently repeats the essence of Elijah's call to serve as God's person. And notice that the angel offers tangible, helpful assistance in the form of physical nourishment, food for the journey and the many perils that still lay ahead.

Please understand that Elijah's crisis is not over as this story ends. His prophetic predicament is not tied up with a neat bow and given a sitcom happy ending. Elijah will drag himself out of bed after this encounter and head out again into the world to try and speak for God, with other Jezebels always around the next turn. Elijah is not promised a trouble-free existence as a messenger of God. He is given non-perishable food for the journey in a world where it's easy to give up and give in to all that's perishable.

The holy meal we share is meant for people like us who are tempted to give in to the depression that often accompanies authentic Christian witness. Holy Communion is not magic. It is not meant to be the equivalent of theological Prozac. But like manna in the wilderness, it is enough. It is non-perishable food in a land filled with junk food. It is food for the journey, the way of the cross that is neither popular nor a path filled with much applause. So hear again the words delivered to a despondent man who once gave up precisely due to troubles brought on by his own faithfulness.

"Get up and eat," says the angel. "Otherwise the journey will be too much for you."

For Reflection and Discussion

- *Prayerfully describe a clinically depressed person you may have befriended in the past. What have you learned from them?*

- *Discuss how prophetic truth-telling might honestly lead to depression in this or any age.*

- *How might we take cues from the angel in this story as we reach out to friends who are depressed?*

IT PLEASED THE LORD THAT SOLOMON HAD ASKED
THIS. . . ." I NOW DO ACCORDING TO YOUR WORD. INDEED
I GIVE YOU A WISE AND DISCERNING MIND." (1 KINGS
3:10, 12)

A Wise and
Discerning Mind

6

1 KINGS 3:3-15

HE WAS THE PRODUCT
of what is perhaps the most
famously illicit sexual tryst
in the entire Bible. Many
attribute a rather provocative scriptural ode of romantic
love to his prosaic writing powers. The impressive temple in Jerusalem, God's house of pilgrimage for many
sojourners over many centuries, was built on his royal watch.
(People still "wail" out prayers to God on the same site.) Proverbs,
pithy snippets of wisdom, poured out of the man like rain falling
on thirsty soil.

His leadership record, however, was a mixed bag—a political alli-
ance with Egypt left him as son-in-law to Pharaoh (perhaps he even
called the man "Dad" at family reunions at their Nile River summer cabin). But just that word—"Egypt"—evoked bad memories of
bondage and brickmaking for the children of Israel. It often matters

whom you marry. Ironically, he would soon order forced conscription and slavery of his own people to achieve his greatest monument to God. Presto, Exodus revisited.

And of course I'm talking about King Solomon, love child of David and Bathsheba, the Bible's most notorious couple. In the chapters just preceding this story from First Kings, Bathsheba slyly finagles the crown for her baby boy. She throws her considerable political weight and beauty around, and soon there is a swearing-in ceremony. We catch up with Solomon in the very early days of his administration. It is night. Solomon is dreaming. And we get to overhear a fairly famous conversation between the neophyte king and God.

I love this scene because it reveals Solomon's vulnerability and his own admission (at least privately) that he doesn't have the foggiest idea how to proceed. We get in a lot of trouble sometimes, pretending to know what we're doing when we really don't. Similar to males like me who push on, utterly lost on a car trip and embarrassed to ask directions, we are sometimes afraid to admit our ignorance and, in the process, make a mess of things. Give the new king some credit. He candidly confesses that he's in way over his head with this new job.

So Solomon admits to God in this dream, "Hey, I don't know how to go out or come in." Loose Hebrew translation: "Help! I don't know my rear end from a hole in the ground." It's a wonderfully faithful prayer to pray before God, pretty much on a daily basis. In those early days of his first term, Solomon was flying by the seat of his pants. He was utterly dependent upon God. And even though that might feel fairly terrifying to all of us, God rather likes this.

When my synodical bishop first contacted me about interviewing to become a pastor in South Carolina, my initial reaction was a quick "no." I was happy in Virginia, serving a wonderful parish for fourteen years. I loved the mountains and loved small towns. We hung up cordially. "Thanks, but no thanks," I told him.

But I got to thinking about the nature of this thing we refer to as "call" in the Bible. (Just to remind you: God's "call" rests upon all baptized people, not just pastors. All Christians are ordained and called into ministry by virtue of holy baptism. More than just folk who go off to seminary have "entered the ministry.") Very often, if a call is authentic, we are called by God not so much to happiness, or a settled life, or a secure and safe predictability. We are often, all of us, called to important tasks for which we feel totally unprepared and completely ill-equipped. And so I eventually said "yes," or maybe it was more of a muffled "okay."

But you know what? I think God *wants* us to confess such a thing. The story in First Kings reveals God's pleasure (3:10) with such a prayer. If we think we've got it all together, a complete handle on our work, on this life, then sometimes we slowly begin to crowd out God—no need for God if we have things so completely under control. That is truly one of the reasons people become inactive in a congregation and sleep in on Sundays. Things seem to be going so very well without God. Will it really matter if I skip a month of Sundays? Miss Holy Communion? What's the big deal?

And so Solomon may have lost his way as his success grew over the years: his power and wealth and prestige, his collusion with things that drew him away from God. Even today in Jerusalem there is a "King Solomon Hotel" in the center of the city. Here's a tantalizing description of the place I gleaned from the web: "All of King Solomon's rooms are luxurious, large and comfortable. The views from the top floors are breathtaking, encompassing the Old City and the historical Tower of David on the west."

King Solomon's aspirations may have been misguided as he aged, but he is surely not alone. These are possibilities for any of us. But here, early on, here in this dream, he got it right. Please notice that God gives him the green light to ask for anything. Now think about that. *Anything.* It's like a genie in the lamp granting you a single wish—anything your heart desires. I won't lie. A few things come to mind for me.

In the second half of the seventeenth century, Luca Giordano, an Italian artist, painted a restless, shirtless, youthful Solomon looking rather buffed, covered in the night only with a sheet. He is tossing and turning, worried, no doubt, about his royal inadequacies. The young king has long hair, curls, bare chest—looking a lot like Brendan Fraser in *George of the Jungle* if you've seen that movie. (Perhaps we need to return to Bibles with color plates to regain adolescent interest in the scriptures.) But it's the depiction of God that arrests my eye in this old painting.

God, with an entourage of angels, is hovering above Solomon's bed. And God looks so pleased, utterly delighted, to be granting Solomon's famous request. "It pleased the Lord," says our story, "that Solomon had asked this." In the painting, a light from God, laser-like, connects directly to the mind of the sleeping king.

Part of what it means to be a follower of Jesus is that we learn over time to ask for and desire the right things. That will also mean learning to admit our inadequacies, our fears, our honesty about feeling less than able to answer the call of God that rests upon each of us.

I don't really know what may be facing you these days that frightens you, perhaps something you know you need to do, but feel utterly ill-equipped to accomplish. But I do know that it pleases God when we bring these fears before him in prayer—to name them aloud and confess our complete dependence upon the Lord for guidance and wisdom.

So when you next kneel at the altar for Holy Communion, hands lifted high to be fed with Christ's body, be reminded that this openness, this asking, this vulnerability, brings pleasure to God, who desires to give us heavenly gifts.

And over time, in ways large and small, we too receive the gift of this young and restless king: a wise and discerning mind.

For Reflection and Discussion

- *Share a time in your past when you've been hesitant to ask for help, pushed on alone, and perhaps made matters worse in the process.*

- *If given a green light to ask for "anything" (like Solomon), what would you request from God in prayer?*

- *Do you agree with this essay's explanation of why many Christians sleep in on Sunday mornings? Why or why not?*

Boating Tips for Night Crossings

MATTHEW 14:13-36

HERE'S A CONVERSATION I sometimes overhear: "You know, how in the world can you Christians be so blindly naïve? Can you honestly tell me with a straight face that you believe some guy actually walked on water, multiplied fish and bread, and calmed storms? Please," they say. "I suppose you've also got some fabulous coastal land to sell me at an unbelievable price. Well, I'm not buying. I left those stories behind back in nursery school."

It's important for the church to take such objections seriously. Our problem, though, in desiring to appear open, non-defensive, and, well, sane, is that we've tripped all over ourselves trying to offer logical explanations for these paranormal, miraculous events of the Bible. And so sometimes we say things like, "Well, you know, people probably brought some food with them that afternoon, a little picnic

213

under their jackets, meager fare. But when Jesus gathered it, blessed and shared it all around, those people had plenty. It was really a miracle of sharing. Everybody was fed because everybody shared." I once heard that at some Lutheran Synod Assembly several years back, four hundred people carefully passed around a single, unglazed doughnut. And because everyone was careful and no one was stingy, all present got a little nibble. Forget hygiene here, I'm trying to explain a miracle.

And so you've got a problem with Jesus walking on water? Do you? Well, you know, *actually* some scholars believe the water was rather shallow. It was windy and all, and those disciples had hardly left the dock. It was pitch-dark out there; those guys were about out of their minds—even thought Jesus was a ghost at first! And so, yeah, I know it *says* that he walked on water, but many think he was actually, well, just wading through it. And you know how we tend to embellish things.

There is a tendency in the church, living in an age where science, by many, is nearly deified, to rationally explain the unexplainable. And so sometimes we unpack a Bible story, remove its obvious bumps, flatten it out in a nice and manageable way, and thereby beat the very life out of it. Is it true? Did it happen just that way? How can we make this odd story accessible and palatable to the discerning masses?

I say let the story stand in all its utter strangeness. The early church told the story this way for a reason. And so instead of posing questions *of* the story (Is it true? Could this happen?), perhaps we should allow the story *to question us*.

Matthew's version of the gospel has a special place for the church. The word "church" is mentioned about eighty times in the New Testament, but only two instances in all four gospels combined, and both of those are in Matthew's version (16:18; 18:15). Church in the Bible is never a place, never a building, but rather always a dynamic, called-out people of God formed in the waters of baptism. Upon rising on Sunday morning and saying, "Wake up, it's time to go to church," we are really uttering a theological absurdity. You cannot "go to church" anymore than you could try and "go to family." Church is not a destination; it's who we are. I have a marvelous magazine article in my office files titled, "Stop Going to Church." I firmly believe that congregational health is about recovering the proper use of this old, familiar word.

In the story under consideration, notice this rather strange biblical line: "Jesus made the disciples get into the boat." He *made* them. This is not an invitational word; coercion is implied. In the previous story, the feeding of all those thousands, it was getting quite dark as the disciples offered their rationale about sending the crowds away. Jesus' nautical instructions fall right on the heels of that massive picnic. If it was getting dark as supper began, well, it's even darker now. And Jesus wants these disciples to huddle together, pile into a boat, and row across a sea in such conditions? I can hear the grumbling. "Get in the boat," he says. "Huddle together. Cast off."

Anne Lamott will tell you without batting an eye: her life was a mess. The best-selling novelist and teacher of writing became dependent on drugs and alcohol at an early age. After college she found herself moving from one bad sexual relationship to another, usually with married men. She eventually became bulimic and almost died.

In her book *Traveling Mercies*, Lamott describes her conversion to Christianity. Raised in a household where her parents scorned religion, she was taught to lampoon and question anything resembling faith in God. She writes of a night in 1984, alone and scared: "I became aware of someone with me, hunkered down in the corner. I knew beyond any doubt that it was Jesus . . . And I was appalled. I thought about my life and my brilliant hilarious progressive friends. I thought about what everyone would think of me if I became a Christian, and it seemed an utterly impossible thing that simply could not be allowed to happen. I turned to the wall and said out loud, 'I would rather die.'"

Her life did not change all at once. She says in an interview: "When I experienced Jesus' presence I didn't want to do anything about it. I just hoped it would pass and that would be the last of it. When it didn't, I still tried to get rid of him. And when I finally said he could come in, it was still a while before I quit drinking and using drugs. My life was still a mess. But I felt maybe the worst was over."[58] Today Anne Lamott is in recovery and doing very well; with her son, she is an active member of a small Presbyterian Church in California.

"Get in the boat," says Jesus. "Huddle together in the dark. Cast off." He *made* them get in. For a Christian, being part of the church is not optional. Of course, being in the boat does not magically protect and inoculate us from storms in this life. The disciples encounter wind and wave pretty quickly that night. Christians have no protective shield to ward off all mishap. We are simply told to congregate and gather, stay together, and Jesus will come with resources to weather any storm. He comes over the water to a people gathered in a boat. The sacramental and liturgical symbolism in this story is far deeper than any dark sea they were crossing.

I suggested earlier that instead of asking endless questions about a story like this one, we should allow the story to question us. And I suppose the story confronts me in my own tendency to try and go it alone—to leave the boat or maybe refuse to get in the boat in the first place. Who has not heard the siren appeal to leave the church? Tired of pettiness and people and particulars, it's often appealing to fly solo spiritually.

So I suppose that's me, not just Peter, wanting to step out of the boat and come to Jesus all by myself, without the sometimes-tiring ballast of the community. Maybe that's you, too, wanting to step out at times. The historic explanation for Peter's sinking is that he just didn't have enough faith. But maybe he sunk because he stepped out of the boat in the first place; he left the community, the church, and tried to make a go of it alone. I find it interesting that once he gets back in the boat with Jesus and the other disciples, the wind ceases. And then they worshipped, right in the bottom of that boat. Worship is what the church does together to find our way in the world.

Long ago, just after feeding thousands and well after nightfall, Jesus made his disciples huddle together in a boat and cross the sea in very uncertain waters.

Jesus came to them in the night, in the storm.
Some advice: stay in the boat.

For Reflection and Discussion

- *How have you tended to "explain" the paranormal miracle stories in the Bible?*

- *Consider the definition of the word "church" in this essay and its possibilities for a new perception of Christian community. What understanding of "church" did you grow up with?*

- *A biblical assumption: it is not possible to grow in Christ apart from a church community. Do you agree or disagree? Why?*

THE EARTH WILL WEAR OUT LIKE A GARMENT, AND THOSE
WHO LIVE ON IT WILL DIE LIKE GNATS. (ISAIAH 51:6)
PRESENT YOUR BODIES AS A LIVING SACRIFICE, HOLY AND
ACCEPTABLE TO GOD. (ROMANS 12:1)

8

Dying Like Gnats

ISAIAH 51:1-8

IF YOU HAVE BEEN
bothered, as I have, by
the 300,000 deaths due
to genocide in the Darfur
region of Sudan in east
Africa—the equivalent of the
entire population of Richland
County, South Carolina, disappear-
ing in violent, planned intentionality over
a span of several years—or the 217,000 who perished in southeast
Asia from the devastating tsunami on the day after Christmas 2004
(a number that makes the *Titanic* look like a minor blip on the radar
screen of human misery), then you will not be comforted with the
reminder that 35,000 people die every day around the world, each
24-hour period, from the effects of malnutrition and hunger.

35,000 per day. That number, blessedly, is going down due to the
tireless efforts of various relief organizations. But the number is still
the equivalent of 350 jets crashing each day, every day, with none of

the hundred passengers on board surviving, which would probably get our collective national attention if that were indeed to occur. It dawned on me not long ago, in the drama that unfolded outside a certain ranch in Texas (a grieving mom protesting the war in Iraq), that I too live in a protective "ranch house" of sorts with many mothers knocking at my door whose cries for attention I summarily ignore.

More numbers: there are now roughly six billion people on the planet at the dawn of a new millennium. Historians estimate that 85 billion people have already preceded us in returning to the soil; half of those were babies and children.[59] All told, approximately fourteen times more dead people than living. Joseph Stalin once coldly said, "One death is a tragedy; a million deaths are a statistic." You don't have to like what he said, but there is a certain ring of truth to it.

∘ ∘ ∘

"Lift up your eyes to the heavens," says the prophet Isaiah to the suffering exiles of Babylon, "and look at the earth beneath; for the heavens will vanish like smoke, the earth will wear out like a garment, and those who live on it will die like gnats."

Those who live on it will die like gnats. You can say what you want about the Bible. And you can offer myriad excuses as to why church people have largely stopped reading it. But my own personal opinion is that the Bible has fallen on hard times because it tries to tell the truth about life and death, whereas we often want to pretend that we'll live forever. Even Easter doesn't make that promise. Easter proclaims a triumph over death, yes, but it doesn't promise that we'll live forever under our own terms—doing exactly what we want eternally. No, Easter leads us to into eternal life under *God's terms*. And if that is true, I suspect some people won't like heaven a whole heck of a lot. The man Jesus, after all, didn't die like a king. He died like a gnat, like so many other gnats of the world. The difference was that he died trusting God, pouring his life out for God, confident of another reality coming this way.

The Bible is absolutely honest about this life. Like gnats, we are here and gone rather quickly, and it's a pretty good bet that we'll encounter our share of pain and suffering along the way. The Bible is unflinchingly candid about telling this truth. Having faith in Jesus, contrary to popular Christian belief, does not insure that we'll have life as we'd like forever—protected, cozy, secure. But something will last forever. Isaiah continues: "Those who live on earth will die like gnats; *but my salvation* will be forever, and my deliverance will never be ended." God's idea of salvation is what we are called to trust, not our own ideas. "Listen to me," God says. "Look to the rock from which you were hewn, and to the quarry from which you were dug." There is something a lot older and deeper mined here than the paper-thin theologies of modern-day America.

So what is God's idea of salvation? And how do we experience it now, in this life, where so many die like gnats?

God's idea of salvation has to do with relinquishment, with giving your whole self over to God—not just your Sunday self, not just that part of yourself that you deem religious, but your whole being, your entire person, those places in your soul where you and only you are now in charge. Someone once said: "A Christian is a person who is prepared to look good on wood."[60] That's relinquishment, conversion; an offering, if you will; a decidedly broader understanding of how we use that word on Sunday morning when we pass around the offering plates. St. Paul says this clearly: "I appeal to you therefore, brothers and sisters, by the mercies of God, to present your bodies as a living sacrifice, holy and acceptable to God, which is your spiritual worship" (Romans 12:1). Listen to how Eugene Peterson puts this same passage in his lively rendering of scripture, *The Message*: "Take your everyday, ordinary life—your sleeping, eating, going-to-work, and walking-around life—and place it before God as an offering." *Present your bodies as a living sacrifice.* Do you see what Paul is inviting us to do here? Let me illustrate.

An altar serves as a focal point of our worship space each week. I do certain holy things at the altar, which often seems like a very mysterious place. "You mustn't touch the altar or play around it in any way," we sometimes tell the children, gravely. "It's holy." And so it is.

But what if I went a little crazy one Sunday and knocked away the candlesticks and missal book and trashed the fair linen? And after that, what if I physically climbed up on the altar and stretched out my body on the holy surface? What would people think? It would be over, wouldn't it? I'd be packing my bags pretty fast, right? Someone would call the bishop, there'd be a series of meetings, and people would start looking for a new pastor. "The last guy went a little crazy one Sunday morning."

But isn't that exactly what Paul has in mind? To offer our bodies as a living sacrifice? Paul is inviting us to not hold back, but to place our *whole selves* into trusting God. And when we do offer this radical trust, something like a death occurs. And it is precisely then that God can get at us and work what the Bible calls "salvation" in our lives—a reality that physical death cannot touch because (surprise!) we've already died.

When we come forward for communion each week we gather near the altar and naturally think of Jesus' ultimate sacrifice. But when we gather at an altar we might also consider our own "living sacrifice" and the offering of our bodies. Next time you stretch up your hands to receive Holy Communion, try to envision your own body stretched out upon the altar up there. "Those who live on the earth will die like gnats; but my salvation will be forever." It is not a matter of *whether* we will give our lives away. The question is how and to whom.

∘ ∘ ∘

A skeptic might say, "Well, what's the use? If we all die like gnats anyway, what difference could it make whether I'm a Christian or not?" It's a good question, an old question. The answer, I think, is that a Christian agrees to go ahead and die early. To stretch out on an altar with Jesus and say, "God, here I am. Take this life I'm offering you." Resurrection, I've noticed, only works on dead people.

You are a *living* sacrifice. Unlike the sacrifices of old, you can get up, jump off the altar of your offering, and move around with some gospel mobility.

Where will you now move? How will you now live in a world where people die like gnats?

God knows.

Here's the plain truth: God wants your body, your life.

All of it.

For Reflection and Discussion

- *What kind of faith are you searching for in a world where so many people die like gnats?*

- *Reflect upon this rather odd statement: "A Christian is a person who is prepared to look good on wood."*

- *What forces are at work in our lives to compartmentalize God into a cozy Sunday slot?*

"THERE IS NOTHING OUTSIDE A PERSON THAT BY GOING IN CAN DEFILE, BUT THE THINGS THAT COME OUT ARE WHAT DEFILE... FOR IT IS FROM WITHIN, FROM THE HUMAN HEART, THAT EVIL INTENTIONS COME." (MARK 7:15, 21)

Internal Life

MARK 7:1-23

IN JESUS' DAY, RELIGIOUS holiness and purity were measured from the outside in. It greatly mattered what you ate and didn't eat, what you touched and didn't touch. There were lots of religious hoops to jump through. Read Leviticus chapter 11 sometime. There you will find a rather exhaustive list of approved and forbidden foods. The Lord is speaking to Moses in this chapter. "[You may eat] any animal that has divided hoofs and is cleft-footed and chews the cud ... But among those that chew the cud or have divided hoofs, you shall not eat the following: *the camel* [which is a great relief to me because I personally think it would be extremely difficult to properly prepare a camel] ... *the rock badger* [I'm also grateful for this particular taboo; the "Thanksgiving Rock Badger" just doesn't haven't the same ring as "Thanksgiving Turkey." Am I right?] ... *and* [finally] *the pig*, for even though it has divided hoofs and is cleft-footed, it does not chew the cud. It is unclean for you." The Word of the Lord.

God then proceeds to approve certain kinds of fish. "Everything in the waters that has fins and scales—such you may eat. But anything in the seas or streams that does not have fins and scales—they are detestable to you *and detestable they shall remain*." (I like the emphasis there.) Leviticus 11 exhaustively spells out the approved menu for God's people. Some birds are okay for outdoor grilling. But the ostrich, the little owl, the great owl, the desert owl, the stork, the bat, and the hoopoe are off limits. We can be thankful for this. The chapter goes on to describe the untouchability of the weasel, gecko, crocodile, and chameleon. Steer clear of these things. Don't you dare touch them, says the Bible. Some of this is just plain common sense if you ask me. For example, you will not find the crocodile in a petting zoo in this or any century.

As you might imagine, these dietary regulations grew into quite an elaborate system of religious do's and don'ts. I'm sure there was a good bit of wiggle room as time went by and corrupt priests received payoffs to let people slide by. This type of religious trafficking wasn't (and isn't) just a Jewish problem, of course. The Christian church has dealt with similar ecclesiastical hoop-jumping in every century of its existence. "This people honors me with their lips," says Jesus, quoting Isaiah, "but their hearts are far from me" (Mark 7:6). Jesus cares nothing for religious show. He's after our hearts. We can say all the right words and show up at all the right times and follow precisely the right religious decorum and still keep God at arm's length. "This people honors me with their lips but their hearts are far from me." It's one of the most devastating things the man ever said.

Wherever people of faith gather, there is a tendency to accentuate the outward manifestation of the faith over a great negligence of the inward. As someone has aptly put it, churches often tend to "major in the minors." We could all probably list several things that seem *absolutely essential* to our faith. But to God, these same "essential" things might be rather peripheral and not very important at all.

So when Jesus called the crowd to him that day, people who knew all about Leviticus 11 and the dietary restrictions and the holy tradition, you can imagine how the religious experts checking up on Jesus from Jerusalem just hit the roof when he said, "Listen to me, all of you; there is nothing outside a person that by going in can defile." Jesus essentially turns an entire religious structure on its head. "The things that come out are what defile," he says. "For it is from within, from the human heart, that evil intentions come." As one modern paraphrase of this verse puts it: "It's not what you swallow that pollutes your life; it's what you vomit—that's the real pollution." Holiness among religious people in Jesus' day consisted of working from the outside in. Jesus completely inverts that notion. He claimed that transformation occurs instead from the inside out.

On one level, we know the truth of this teaching. We know that a person doesn't just wake up one morning and say, "Well now, this is a fine day to commit adultery." No. Most human mistakes are normally hatched over time, considered and debated in the human heart long before they're acted upon. That's basically true of everything on Jesus' list in Mark 7:21-22. Evil is normally not spontaneous. This is as true of garden-variety slander as it is of a plot to bomb a mosque in Iraq while innocent people are worshipping. Evil is hatched over time in the human heart. There are exceptions to this, I'm sure, but those exceptions are rare. Evil, with all its many faces, takes hold in our hearts long before we actually do it. That's why any attempted legislation of an outward morality will always fail. Even as we celebrated the 40th anniversary of Dr. King's famous speech and the strides our country has made in civil rights for all, it is still strikingly painful to note that all the laws in the wide world cannot change racist hearts. "It is from within, from the human heart that evil intentions come."

Jesus had this right. And what's more, I think we agree with him. Please forgive me, then, for asking a few pointed questions. If what Jesus is saying is true, then why do we seem so concerned about our outward reputations, our visible exteriors? To put this another way: If "all evil" comes from "within" (and, by the way, I also think the converse is true: all good), then why do I spend so much time on my yard, my home, my body, my things, and so little time on my prayer and devotional life? What would impel me to spend two hours waxing my car and two minutes the same day in prayer? "For it is from within, from the human heart, that evil intentions come." We know the truth in this statement. But here's the bottom line: even though I know where evil comes from (you go, Jesus: you tell those Pharisees a thing or two), even though I know this, I must think deep down that evil mostly comes from others, given a quick comparison of all the exterior stuff that grabs my attention compared to the great neglect of my interior life.

There is a large unseen landscape within every single person in the world, a landscape that God seeks to claim and transform. We cannot live for Jesus until we give him full access there. I'm talking about your inner life—the territory within us all that we become aware of when we're alone, when the TV is shut off, when our noisy lives are silenced. It is home for our uncensored thoughts that never get spoken out loud. Stuff happens in this place that you don't even tell your spouse or best friend.

If people had direct access to this life that we don't show, even the tip of its hidden iceberg, then we'd all be embarrassed, ashamed, and possibly in jail. This is the place where dreams and anger and addiction and lust and hope and envy and a thousand positive and negative forces in us are constantly at war. And here's the thing: if Jesus doesn't enter this landscape on a regular basis (and we are masters at keeping him out), then it is very easy to live out this life on the basis of whatever outer image grabs our attention and distracts us.

In the final book of C. S. Lewis's classic series *The Chronicles of Narnia*, Lucy stands with an old friend, the Faun Tumnus, and looks over the wall of a garden. They look down and see all of Narnia spread out before them. "But when you looked down," writes Lewis, "you found that this hill was much higher than you had thought: it sank down with shining cliffs, thousands of feet below them and trees in that lower world looked no bigger than grains of green salt." Lucy moves away from the wall and turns inward to look again at the garden. "'I see,' she said at last, thoughtfully. 'I see now. This garden . . . is far bigger inside that it was outside.' 'Of course, Daughter of Eve,' said the Faun. 'The further up and the further in you go, the bigger everything gets. The inside is larger than the outside.'"[61]

Jesus said, "It is from within, from the human heart" that schemes are hatched and all human evil finds a home. I think we know the truth of this teaching. But it's still shocking to me how much time I spend fretting over the externals—stuff that really, in the long run, doesn't matter much.

If Jesus is right, and surely he is, our neglect of the inner life (compared to our culture's unhealthy obsession with the outer) powerfully reveals the advent of a national spiritual crisis. We are a people drowning in mail-order catalogs offering every conceivable tonic to reshape our outer realities. Jesus has named the territory for true conversion. If our problems come "from within," then so do the solutions. No incarcerated prisoner, no recovering drug addict, no shaky marriage, and no troubled young person will find peace until learning to navigate the waters of the inner life. We know deep down that such a statement is true, And yet even churches only scratch the surface of offering people ways to develop this inner life and turn off the outer noise. "Lord, teach us to pray," said the early disciples. According to Jesus, it's the very place to begin.

William Willimon once said, "Every congregation is a congregation of sinners. As if that weren't bad enough, they all have sinners for pastors." We are all a messy jumble of greed, lust, anger, hypocrisy, and all sorts of garden-variety garbage. How do we change? In Jesus' day, people believed that holiness was maintained from the *outside in*. Avoid rock badgers and fried ostrich, and you were home free. Jesus knew such beliefs were naïve. True lasting change occurs from the *inside out*, within the human heart.

We can fake it for an hour or so per week with all the right words. If we seek true and lasting transformation, however, Jesus invites us to go deeper.

For Reflection and Discussion

- *Why do you think we sometimes become overly concerned with the external ("how things look") compared to the demotion of our concern with the internal?*

- *If transformation does indeed occur from "the inside out," what suggestions for a spiritual curriculum might you offer those in your congregation responsible for adult formation and education?*

- *Respond to this sentence from the essay: "If Jesus doesn't enter this [inner] landscape on a regular basis, then it is very easy to live out this life on the basis of whatever outer image grabs our attention and distracts us."*

TRULY, YOU ARE TO ME LIKE A DECEITFUL BROOK, LIKE
WATERS THAT FAIL. (JEREMIAH 15:18)

Reply from the Deceitful Brook

JEREMIAH 15:10-21

I THINK IT'S very important to pay special attention when anyone sasses God in the Bible, talks back to the Lord. Job really lets loose on God as you may recall in that famous book about the mystery of suffering. And Jonah, after climbing out of the belly of a big fish, sounds off before God and goes off on a big pout. Remember why? Jonah was upset that God was merciful to people who really didn't deserve his mercy. I've been there; you have, too.

Lots of people sass Jesus in the New Testament. One of my favorite scenes is where the neighbors of Lazarus, Jesus' good family friend, gather around the grave after Lazarus dies from an illness. The neighbors say, "Couldn't this guy who made a blind man see have kept our friend from dying?" It's a pretty sassy thing to say out loud to Jesus, but it's honest. Who honestly hasn't wondered something similar? "If Jesus did *that*, then why can't he do this over here?"

There are more than a handful of these rather uppity retorts to God in the Bible. And I have to admit I rather like them—they give us a green light to be utterly honest with God in prayer, to not hold back, to stop being so mannerly and proper in our prayerful address. God's got big shoulders. God can take it. Let 'er rip.

One of my favorite examples of prayerful sassiness is from the book of Jeremiah. The prophet first reviews his own faithfulness and where that's gotten him. "Lord, you know what I've been through," Jeremiah begins. "Remember me in my exhaustion. Please don't leave me alone here with these people. I'm doing all this for you, Lord, so it only seems fair that you kick the rear ends of all my enemies. Really stick it to them, Lord. You know they all deserve it. Look, I did everything you told me to do. I followed your word and never went to wild parties. I sat alone on Friday nights. I feel so completely alone and never have any fun. Nobody understands me, Lord. Why won't this pain go away? Am I supposed to feel this way forever? *Where are you God?* You know what you remind me of sometimes, Lord? You're like a mountain stream, a deceitful brook that never has any water in it. It's feast or famine with you. You've failed me" (15:15-18, author's paraphrase).

I remember hiking the Appalachian Trail in Pennsylvania many years ago during a very hot summer; we were dangerously low on water. The trail in that state follows a series of long rocky ridges. To get water you have to leave the ridge and hike steeply down to a spring. It was depressing one hot afternoon to find a completely dry spring and then hike steeply back up to the main trail, knowing that a few swallows of water would have to last until evening. Jeremiah compares God to that occasional spring.

Now that's a prayer we don't hear very often, at least not in church. But it's right there in the Bible. An editor could have chopped it out, pressed the ancient scribal "delete key," but it made the cut and you know, I'm glad it's there. Jeremiah has reached the end of his rope and so he dares to offer prayerful impertinence to God; he talks back to God with brazen sass. And I'm guessing that God prefers this honesty over occasional pious platitudes mouthed out of unthinking habit before meals or sleep.

So that's one truth at work in this old Bible story—let 'er rip. God can take the honest prayer. But there is an interesting "Part Two" embedded in this same passage. Jeremiah lets fly and concludes his prayer to God with that honest line about a deceitful brook, a dry spring. But then we get to hear God's reply. I know that it seems like we're speaking into thin air sometimes in prayer and that no one appears to be listening, but in the Bible prayer is never a monologue, always a dialogue. And so God answers Jeremiah. It's a strange answer.

Now you would think here that God would throw a big, fatherly arm around Jeremiah's slumping shoulders and comfort the poor wretch. The prophet has had a hard day, a hard life. He's been out there on the western front speaking up for what is right, and he seems on the verge of tears. You would at least expect a "there, there now" from God and perhaps a big reassuring bear hug. That's what God does best, isn't it?

If you happen to make it onto a quiz show sometime in the future and Alex Trebek asks the contestants to list several popular adjectives to describe the Lord God Almighty, then I have a suspicion you might hit your buzzer with confidence and offer these: *loving, supportive, helpful, kind, understanding.* Always understanding and always there, perpetually ready to affirm and bless. And all in the audience would nod in agreement and Alex would say, "Show 'em what they've won, Johnny."

But somewhere in the audience I see this hand of protest. If Jeremiah attended quiz shows I think he might offer another set of adjectives to describe God. For God refuses to coddle Jeremiah even though he seems like a perfect candidate for coddling. God refuses to support Jeremiah with the type of support Jeremiah feels is his rightly due. God, apparently, is nobody's teddy bear. "If you turn back, I'll take you back," says God. "If you utter what is precious, and not what is worthless, you shall serve as my mouth." God goes on to say, "I will make you to this people a fortified wall of bronze; they will fight against you, but they shall not prevail against you." In other words, says God, *this is more about me than you.*

Sassing, talking-back to God, is tolerated in the Bible, but there are apparently limits to sassing. God is always ready to welcome us back, but on his terms, not ours.

Our culture blesses, affirms, and supports people who engage in almost any behavior, however sinful. Garret Keizer suggests that we have a new Golden Rule: "Thou shalt always be supportive."[62] It is hard for us to engage in loving, confrontational speech with one another. We don't want to sound (heaven forbid) judgmental. So we throw an arm around any behavior and say, "I understand. Of course I want to support you." And sometimes that's exactly what we need in church life. But sometimes such so-called support is not what we need. Sometimes we need to tell the hard truth to each other. "And it's the truth," says Jesus, "that will set you free."

Several centuries after Jeremiah's prayer, a certain disciple of Jesus sidles up and tries to throw a caring arm around our Lord's shoulder. Jesus has just foretold his future destiny, what's about to happen down the road in Jerusalem. "This must never happen to you," says the loving and affirming disciple. "God forbid what you're describing." Peter was only trying to be supportive and helpful.

So Jesus' reply may seem a little harsh. My heavens, Jesus even says these supportive ideas are *satanic* (Mark 8:33). Jesus doesn't sound at all understanding or loving or kind, or like any of the adjectives we normally assign to him (and neither did God, you'll recall, in his response to Jeremiah).

But perhaps what Peter needed most at that moment was not coddling. Perhaps what this disciple needed most was the truth. We badly need to rediscover this sort of speech in the church.

For the truthful word can often be the most loving word.

For Reflection and Discussion

- *How do you feel about offering "prayerful impertinence" to God?*

- *Why do we need a God who does more in our lives than offer support and affirmation?*

- *Without breaking a confidence, share a time when someone told you a truthful, loving word that was difficult to hear at the time.*

11

All Things Considered

COLOSSIANS 1:13-20

TO HAVE FAITH THAT there is a God in a world like ours sometimes requires a lot of hard work and imagination. In our world a lot can happen to shake our faith, leaving us wondering if there really is a God who cares about the intimate, personal, daily details of our lives in a way we would like. Who hasn't flirted with what a close friend of mine once wrote in a letter. "If there is a God in a world like ours," he wrote, "God does not deserve our respect. If He can change things and doesn't or won't, then I choose not to respect him." Faith sometimes requires a lot of hard work and imagination. "Life is difficult," wrote M. Scott Peck in the first three words of his best-selling book *The Road Less Traveled.*[63] For those who keep their eyes open in the world, so is faith.

But lately I'm just as convinced of another truth. I'm just as convinced that *non-faith* is difficult. Maintaining trust in a loving God in a world like ours is indeed challenging, yes. But maintaining disbelief in God in a world like ours is also no walk in the park. What I'm trying to say is this: every morning that a Christian opens the front page of the newspaper or listens to the evening news or walks into the local intensive care unit is a lot like opening the book of Job. Our faith is challenged and a voice we attempt to suppress starts the whisperings all over again. Bald atheism has its own siren appeal. But those who give up God because "he does not deserve our respect" due to various and sundry sufferings (as my friend puts it) are not quite off the hook, for there's still quite a bit of explaining to do, at least as much mystery and head-scratching without God as with. Give up God and you've still got facts like these with which to contend.

"The nuclear weak force," I recently read, "is ten times the strength of gravity. Had the weak force been slightly weaker, all the hydrogen in the universe would have been turned to helium (making water impossible, for example)."[64] I have no idea what the nuclear weak force is or does, but I'm fairly thankful for water and know why we need it. Apparently, that we have water at all involves something more than just luck. Another conundrum to consider: "If the difference between a proton and a neutron were not exactly as it is—roughly twice the mass of an electron—then all neutrons would have become protons or vice-versa. Say good-bye to chemistry as we know it," says my source, "and to life."[65] It's been a while since I took chemistry, but I don't think you have to be on a first-name basis with subatomic particles or their respective mathematical ratios to appreciate being alive and how we almost weren't. Apparently, that we have life at all involves something more than random chance. It's a rather narrow window of scientific possibility we're talking about here.

Given the world we live in, it might be something of a relief to give up God. I'm not denying that. But giving up God doesn't get one off the cosmological hook. Living *with* God is a lot of work. But so is living *without*. There's still a lot of explaining to do. And I haven't even asked you to make comprehensible the existence of wild columbine or giraffes or indigo bunting or the undying affection of my faithful dog, Bonnie.

In his beautiful letter to the Colossians, St. Paul is making some bodacious claims about Jesus that we normally don't assign to him. Most Christians are rather parochial about their prayer concerns and tend to pray the way writer Anne Lamott prays. She says that most Christian prayers, including her own, tend to be offered in two simple formats: a) "Thank you, thank you, thank you" or, b) "Help me, help me, help me."

Now while the Bible certainly suggests that God hears such prayers, Paul's letter describes a far larger job description for Jesus than we normally expect from even him. Paul's Christ is one who is concerned with "all things." Everything from the supernova to the faithful prayer whine. (We all petition Christ with what amounts to what I call a "theological hangnail" at times. He smiles and indulges us.) Paul says Christ reigns over "all things"—everything from the obvious to the subtle, from the ridiculous to the sublime. He is Lord of all.

"Praise to the Lord," a famous hymn gushes, "who o'er *all things* is wondrously reigning." The phrase is repeated no less than five times by Paul in just a handful of verses from Colossians. "For in him *all things* in heaven and earth were created, things visible and invisible, whether thrones or dominions or rulers or powers—*all things* have been created through him and for him. He himself is before *all things*, and in him *all things* hold together." Many think this part of Paul's letter is a fragment of an early Christian hymn. If so, the repeated refrain is rather obvious.

Unfortunately, many Christians pretend not to know this song. Or we choose to sing only selected verses. It is so easy to make Jesus Lord of some things but not all things. It's tempting to box Jesus in and limit his Lordship to my situation, this present moment, and a certain slice of South Carolina. Surely he smiles more on the United States than on other nations, doesn't he? Surely he loves Christians more than non-Christians, agree?

This is a tremendously threatening song for most people. And if you dare to sing along, it will severely stretch the commonly understood nature of the work of Christ. Our problem is that our perception of Christ's mission is usually too small. Is Christ only at work among churches? Among Christians? Keep going. Among humans? On this planet? Do something for me. Try capturing Christ. Try pinning him down. Limit his sway. As someone has said, "Try slapping God on the back. You'll miss."

This is such an important hymn for us to sing. A common set of concerns for Christians living in the twenty-first century deals with questions such as, "Well, where is Christ in *my* life? This or that personal situation? An important upcoming decision?" Fair questions, all. But this old hymn from Colossians pushes us towards another set of questions that don't get asked as often. Namely: What is Christ up to in our community? In our country? In the world? God doesn't see this earth through the eyes of Rand-McNally.

Many, many Christians have an underdeveloped Christology, a stunted picture of Jesus that gets stuck in a "me and Him" mode and never matures. Jesus certainly works that way but if we never move beyond it, the church's work is severely restricted to the felt needs of its members, and the role of Christ in our lives is limited to the merely personal: my needs, my situation, my kin.

I don't disagree with this statement: to have faith that there is a God in a world like ours sometimes requires a lot of hard work and imagination. But I've come to know something. My faith tends to fluctuate according to a rather fickle spiritual barometer, the ups and downs of my own little life. Maybe this is your story, too. I so often need a much larger perspective of God to shake me out of the personal stupor I happen to be in.

I'm convinced this helps: "All things have been created through him and for him." *All things.* To believe that does not explain away all our faith difficulties. But widening the territory of Christ's dominion reminds me that faith is not just my personal ticket to heaven or my promise of a pain-free life.

Faith is trust that as Christ reigns in love over all things, I will be counted among the things he loves—along with you, with many others, with corners of the cosmos we cannot begin to fathom. "All things have been created through him and for him" (Colossians 1:16).

If this is true, we may find ourselves kneeling and offering praise and thanksgiving in some very unexpected places.

For Reflection and Discussion

- *Discuss this statement from the essay: "Living with God is a lot of hard work. But so is living without."*

- *How does a wider understanding of Christ's work as Lord of "all things" affect the common "me and God" theological posture that never matures?*

- *"God doesn't see this earth through the eyes of Rand-McNally." What does this statement mean to you?*

JACOB WAS LEFT ALONE; AND A MAN WRESTLED WITH HIM UNTIL DAYBREAK. (GENESIS 32:24)

THREE WORDS CAPTURE **Nocturnal River Wrestling**
my attention in this famous
Old Testament passage. The
first word is *night*. A lot can
happen at night. Darkness GENESIS 32:1-32
falls and sleep does or does not
descend upon us. Small matters
loom large in the darkness. Noises and
worries amplify. There is something about
the night that is completely out of our control. Disturbing dreams
arrive uninvited. Past indiscretions creep out of the closet. Sinister
plans are hatched in dim light. My brother-in-law's father used to
demand a strict high school curfew, even on Friday nights, "because
nothing good ever happens after midnight," he would say.

Something woke Jacob up that night so long ago. He couldn't
sleep, which is a little surprising for a man who once used a stone for
a pillow (Genesis 28:11). You'd think Jacob, of all people, could sleep
through anything. Was something bothering Jacob? What was it?

239

We can probably make an educated guess about what causes Jacob's insomnia. Jacob is heading home after many years away. Remember why he left home in the first place? Jacob, with his mother's conniving assistance, cheated his older brother Esau out of both blessing and birthright. Jacob even super-glued animal hair to his smooth arms, duping his blind dad, shamelessly lying to an old bedfast man in order to snatch the rightful place of the eldest son. Jacob comes by his name honestly. His name in Hebrew means "cheater." Jacob had to run away from home to escape the murderous threats of his livid older brother.

But now, years later, Jacob is heading home. Maybe he was coming to terms with what a jerk he had been, decided to enroll in an early twelve-step program, and had reached the step of reconciliation; only one way to do that—face his brother. And there is really no reason to believe that the sibling fury has waned after all these years. Early in this same chapter we learn that Esau is only a day away, accompanied by four hundred men. And upon hearing that, Jacob perhaps rethinks this "twelve-step" stuff but certainly does two things that probably any of us might do when backed into a corner: first he prays and then he appeases.

Hear this prayer of a con-artist trying to reform. After acknowledging God's might and his own unworthiness, Jacob prays: "Deliver me, please, from the hand of my brother, from the hand of Esau, for I am afraid of him; he may come and kill us all, the mothers with the children" (32:11). It's an honest prayer, even if it is delivered from a foxhole. Amusing, and rather true to character, is the lavish appeasement that Jacob adds to the prayer. By my count, he then sends over five hundred animals on ahead as a gift—an assortment of goats, sheep, camels, cows, and donkeys. Prayer is one thing. But just to be sure, send a love offering, a little gift. It certainly can't hurt.

So, yes, on this night before their meeting, it's safe to say that Jacob had a tough time sleeping. Maybe he felt guilty after all these years. But I'm guessing the emotion that really wakes him up is fear. Had any night fears lately? They come creeping out after dark, don't they? That's the first word: *night*.

The second word is *river*. Our story suggests that Jacob went to bed that night and maybe even fell asleep for a while. But then for some reason he got up, took down the tent, packed up all of his belongings, and crossed the river in the pitch black with his whole family and a complete menagerie of farm animals. It must have been quite a sight—a squawking, mooing, complaining clatter of noise in what was perhaps a moonless navigation. "Where are we going, Daddy? What time is it?" the trusting child must have asked, rubbing sleep from her eyes. Have you ever forded a river at night? It's hard enough to feel the bottom with your feet in daylight. Jacob's family pitches camp on the other side and settles down again for the night, but then our hero does a curious thing. Jacob leaves his family on the far side of the river, and then crosses back over to the original campsite. Who knows what time it is by now, but Jacob stretches out again under the stars, all alone. I'd say he's at least a little damp after all these wet crossings. Maybe he wanted to be alone with his thoughts, not knowing what tomorrow would bring, his brother only a couple of miles away.

On a deep, psychological level, rivers represent a border between one land and another. The Bible is absolutely laden with river imagery—the rivers running through Eden, the rivers of Babylon where God's people sat down to weep, the river flowing out of the temple in Ezekiel and again in Revelation, symbolizing restoration and God's abiding permanence. When considering a river anywhere in the Bible, or even the three running through my own city (the Broad, Saluda, and Congaree), a Christian might think of baptism—Jesus' in the Jordan, or ours in the waters running through any local font of life. Jacob's lonely night beside the Jabbok pre-dates Christian baptism, of course, but such a wet setting still makes this story absolutely pregnant with sacramental possibility. Jacob, a conniving cheater, tosses and turns on the banks of a river, the very place where God restores and makes all things new.

The next time you have a hard time sleeping because of something you've done in your past, you might consider wandering down in the dark to the building where your church congregates. Let yourself in and camp out right beside the font. It's where God restores "conniving cheaters" like you and me. That's the second word: *river*. Amazing things happen beside them in the Bible.

And now we come to a third word, and perhaps you've already guessed it. The third word is *wrestling*. Have you ever camped out alone in the middle of nowhere? You hear and even see strange things alone in the darkness. I was camping in Maine many years ago, heading south on the Appalachian Trail on my way to Georgia. Completely alone in my small tent on a very still night, reading a book by candlelight, I suddenly heard what must have been a very large moose crashing through the underbrush. It scared the heaven out of me.

Jacob is alone at night beside the river and a figure crashes out of the shadows and tries to break his neck. This is no friendly wrestling match—the sweating and the grunting and maybe the cursing last until dawn. The interpretive history of Jacob's opponent is interesting—nobody is quite sure who the other wrestler is. Jacob later says, "I have striven with God *and* with humans." Well, which is it?

And that is precisely the ambiguous beauty of this story. In the night shadows, beside the waters of our birth, our wrestling always involves both God *and* others—hardly ever just one or the other. Some say the opponent is an angel, others say God, still others claim Esau himself has jumped his brother. I say maybe it's all three grappling in the dust in this watery night struggle between heaven and earth.

Wrestling will always be an important part of our faith life. We may want God to be our best pal, our closest chum who turns a blind eye to all behavior, but God knows better. God knows that real change cannot occur from a supportive pat on the back, a divine "there, there now." Real change is born in the crucible of wrestling, a hard-fought battle of wills. If your faith life is completely void of all wrestling, I might wonder about you. Growth in faith will always cost us something—we might even be left with a limp.

Morning arrives and Jacob is a changed man. Everything about him has changed—his name, the way he walks, even the way he is now prepared to meet his older brother. (By the way, that meeting goes well for Jacob. It's in the next chapter if you want to look it up.)

I hope you see by now that this ancient story is really both old and new. It's certainly about Jacob, a conniving cheat who tosses and turns beside a river and is jumped by God one night. But it's also about you and me, conniving cheats all around, who drag the past so regularly into the present—insomniacs with a fearful conscience.

As with Jacob there is also hope for us. For there is One who walked this earth, whose Spirit absolutely permeates our world even still. He too will jump us from the shadows, and upset the many ways we keep him at a distance. He is more than our good friend. He will never let us go, we who are experts at slipping away.

Night. River. Wrestle. Remember those three words. And remember the One who meets us in the night beside the water, wrestling with us until we are ready to meet the past and face the future, wholly forgiven and forever changed.

For Reflection and Discussion

- *Think of a specific person with whom you've had a falling out—a situation that may still be awaiting reconciliation. Are there elements in this old Bible story that might speak to your own situation? How?*

- *Consider the three central words in this essay as applied to the story of Jacob and Esau—night, river, wrestling. Which of these three words applies most to your emerging faith? Why?*

- *What do you make of the interpretive possibility that Jacob's wrestling partner may be a variety of human and divine opponents?*

Notes

1. Burton L. Visotsky, *Reading the Book: Making the Bible a Timeless Text* (New York: Schocken, 1991), 18.

2. Thomas Merton, *Opening the Bible* (Philadelphia: Fortress Press, 1970), 14.

3. Deuteronomy 6:4-9 reads: "Hear, O Israel: the LORD is our god, the LORD alone. You shall love the LORD your God with all your heart, and with all your soul, and with all your might. Keep these words that I am commanding you today in your heart. Recite them to your children and talk about them when you are at home and when you are away, when you lie down and when you rise. Bind them as a sign on your hand, fix them as an emblem on your forehead, and write them on the doorposts of your house and on your gates."

4. C. S. Lewis, *The Silver Chair* (New York: Collier, 1980), 21.

5. Reynolds Price, *The Tongues of Angels* (New York: Ballantine, 1990), 67.

6. It will be very helpful to keep a modern translation of the Bible close at hand while reading this book. The parameters of each Bible story are noted at the heading of each essay. A benefit of this exercise will be to increase your familiarity with a book that can feel befuddling in its overall breadth.

7. Juan Williams, "Nelson Mandela, out of Bondage," in *Washington Post*, June 1990.

8. I'm drawing here upon the work of Marva Dawn in her book, *A Royal "Waste" of Time: The Splendor of Worshiping God and Being Church for the World* (Grand Rapids: Eerdmans, 1999). She cites C. S. Lewis in her chapter titled "Why Is a Catechumenal Process Needed in Contemporary Culture?" (see especially 240–41).

9. Barbara Brown Taylor, "Endangered Language," in *Christian Century*, December 6–13, 2000, 1,276.

10. Perry Garfinkel, "Buddha Rising: Out of the Monastery, into the Living Room," *National Geographic*, December 2005, 88–109.

11. Arthur Miller, *Death of a Salesman* (New York: Viking, 1949), 138.

12. Philip Yancey, "The Visited Planet," in *Watch for the Light: Readings for Advent and Christmas* (Farmington: Plough, 2001), 256–57.

13. Adapted from Charles Frazier, *Cold Mountain* (New York: Atlantic Monthly Press, 1997), 107.

14. Frederick Buechner, "Vocation," in *Wishful Thinking: A Seeker's ABC*, revised edition (Harper & Row, 1993), 118–19.

15. See Will Campbell's marvelous book, *Brother to a Dragonfly* (New York: Continuum, 1977), for a moving and detailed narrative of a southern white pastor's role in the civil rights movement.

16. First Kings 17:1-16.

17. Second Kings 5:1-19.

18. See my book *Preaching to Skeptics and Seekers* (Nashville: Abingdon, 2001), 86–90.

19. Lewis B. Smedes, *The Art of Forgiving* (New York: Ballantine, 1996), 7.

20. Ibid., 8.

21. Eugene Peterson et al., eds., *Subversive Spirituality* (Grand Rapids: Eerdmans, 1997), 27.

22. Elizabeth O'Connor, *Call to Commitment* (New York: Harper & Row, 1963), 34, 38.

23. Ronald G. Luckey, Faith Lutheran Church, Lexington, Kentucky.

24. Dallas Willard, *The Spirit of the Disciplines: Understanding How God Changes Lives* (San Francisco: Harper & Row, 1988), 152.

25. Stephanie Paulsell, "Honoring the Body," in *Practicing Our Faith: A Way of Life for a Searching People*, edited by Dorothy C. Bass (San Francisco: Jossey-Bass, 1997), 19.

26. Jim Crace, *Quarantine* (New York: Picador, 1998), 157.

27. C. S. Lewis, *The Screwtape Letters* (New York: Bantam, 1982), 19–20.

28. Mark Twain, *Letters from the Earth* (New York: Harper & Row, 1962), 41–42.

29. Eugene H. Peterson, *Leap over a Wall: Earthy Spirituality for Everyday Christians* (San Francisco: Harper & Row, 1997), 187.

30. Reynolds Price, *The Good Priest's Son* (New York: Scribner, 2005), 110.

31. Barbara Brown Taylor, *Speaking of Sin: The Lost Language of Salvation* (Boston: Cowley, 2000), 46.